Praise for *Mindful Parent Happy Child*

"Dr. Placone's remarkably insightful and practical book on Mindful Parenting can transform the daily minutia and frustrations of parenting into a path of transformation. Her book is a particular treasure for parents struggling to find balance among the conflicting demands of family life, offering specific methods for slowing down, making thoughtful decisions, and gaining access to inner wisdom about what really matters in one's life."
—JOE BAVONESE, PH.D., LICENSED PSYCHOLOGIST,
DIRECTOR OF THE RELATIONSHIP INSTITUTE

"A masterful combination of theory and practice, this book will benefit parents, teachers, and all those who engage with children. This is a book that will be passed from one reader to another, parents and professionals alike."
—SHARI DELISLE, PH.D., FOUNDER, EDUCATOR OF KIDS' TURN,
AND COOPERATIVE PARENTING

"I would highly recommend this book to both parents and professionals. The title says everything you need to know about how this dynamic approach delivers in a way that can truly change lives."
—MOON KERSON, PH.D., ADJUNCT FACULTY, PHILLIPS GRADUATE
INSTITUTE. FORMER RESEARCH FACULTY AT SANTA BARBARA
GRADUATE INSTITUTE

"Dr. Placone has done a brilliant job in weaving the diverse fields of parenting, mindfulness, and interpersonal neurobiology into a user-friendly parenting book—for anyone with or working with children."
—WILLIAM ROLFE PH.D., LICENSED PSYCHOLOGIST. ADJUNCT FACULTY,
PHILLIPS GRADUATE INSTITUTE

"Drawing on the mindfulness research of Daniel Siegel, M.D., Jack Kornfield, Ph.D., and Jon Kabat-Zinn, Ph.D., as well as her own teaching, Pilar Placone, Ph.D. artfully presents her integrated vision of mindful parenting. *Mindful Parent Happy Child* is presented in a concise, reader-friendly format. Anyone wishing to transform his or her parenting approach will benefit from reading her work. Highly recommended for therapists as well."
—SHERRY HARTLWELL, LMFT, FOUNDER, EARLIEST RELATIONSHIPS NETWORK

"I can think of few challenges in life more complex and more important than being a good mom or dad. In this powerful but gentle book, Dr. Pilar Placone reminds us that the same skills that go into being an effective parent also serve to make us effective *humans*, mindfully aware of our power to influence and our power to choose. Dr. Placone provides kind support, generous advice, and thoughtful paths of self-exploration that will lead to better parenting, stronger families, healthier relationships, and happier kids. I hope everyone with a child will read this book!"
—MICHAEL D. YAPKO, PH.D., CLINICAL PSYCHOLOGIST AND AUTHOR OF *MINDFULNESS, AND HYPNOSIS, AND DEPRESSION IS CONTAGIOUS*

"*Mindful Parent Happy Child* offers parents powerful tools for self-nurturing so that they can provide a secure, mind/heart building base for their children. These wise words invite all those who care for children into a supportive space. The book is filled with practical suggestions for parents to connect with themselves and their young ones. A wonderful gift for both new and seasoned parents!"
—BONNIE BADENOCH, PH.D., CO-FOUNDER OF NURTURING THE HEART WITH THE BRAIN IN MIND

"This book is transformational for the parent who desires to have a deeper connection with their child—essential in fostering a secure attachment so their child thrives in life. As a Clinical Child Psychologist working in a busy U.K. Children's Service, I can't wait to start sharing these principles and strategies with the parents I work with!"
—DR. ANGEL ADAMS, CLINICAL PSYCHOLOGIST (LONDON, ENGLAND)

MINDFUL PARENT
HAPPY CHILD
A Guide to Raising Joyful
and Resilient Children

MINDFUL PARENT
HAPPY CHILD
A Guide to Raising Joyful
and Resilient Children

Pilar M. Placone, Ph.D.

alaya press
www.AlayaPress.net

Alaya Press™
601 Chimalus Drive
Palo Alto, CA 94306
www.alayapress.net

10 9 8 7 6 5 4 3 2
First edition published 2011
Printed in the United States on SFI certified sustainable paper

Library of Congress Cataloging In Publication Data
Placone, Pilar M.
Mindful Parent Happy Child: A Guide to Raising Joyful and Resilient Children
Includes bibliographical references
ISBN-10: 0-615-35878-0
ISBN-13: 978-0-615-35878-9
1. Parenting   2. Child rearing   3. Psychology
4. Interpersonal Neurobiology 5. Meditation
2010904114

Cover photo by Michael Paul Franklin
Cover & book design by CenterPointe Media
www.CenterPointeMedia.com

For
Ian and Claire
Your loving acceptance has brought me far.

And for
My husband, Frank
You inspire me every day.

Contents

Chapter Five: **Maintaining and Deepening the Connection**

Chapter Six: **The Workbook: A Six-Week Class for You**

Chapter Seven: **The Seeds We Sow Become the Garden We Grow**

....

Foreword

In the modern times we live in, raising children has become a challenge. With two working parents in many homes, an explosion of electronic media (that now has three-year-olds asking for cell phones), and the stress and hurry of the present-day family, the idea of raising "joyful and resilient children" may seem like a poorly timed joke! Yet, we also are in a time when we know an awful lot about how parenting affects or entrains biology and creates secure attachment, which has *everything* to do with happiness and resiliency.

In fact, the quality of the parent/child relationship—particularly during the sensitive period of right-hemisphere development (last trimester of pregnancy to about two and a half to three years)—is what lays the foundation for secure, versus insecure, socioemotional development. In other words, "good-enough" parenting leads to children who

Since we were all emotionally entrained by our parents or others who raised us, our own emotional reactivity is often the hidden explosion awaiting an interaction with someone who cannot perceive that we are stressed and in need of a moment to ourselves.

are secure and have emotional regulation, which in turn leads to happier, more resilient children. To get there, however, requires "good-enough" emotional regulation in the parent.

Dr. Placone is well aware of how parenting affects brain development, which is why she focuses her work on "Mindful Parenting." Since we were all emotionally entrained by our parents, or others who raised us, our own emotional reactivity is often a hidden explosion waiting for an interaction with someone who cannot perceive that we are stressed and in need of a moment to ourselves. Of course, children fall into this category ... regularly.

Dr. Placone provides a parenting program that uses effective tools to increase a parent's mental flexibility and resiliency while parenting. The real strength of her work is including children through all developmental stages. She gives many relevant examples of how to "rehearse" a difficult parent/child interaction. Her focus on repairing a stressful interaction or comment we wished we hadn't made is completely in tune with regulation theory.

Dr. Placone's focus on making oneself available to children, honoring yet balancing our own internal feelings, and becoming mindful of how we tend to handle conflict are all in accord with becoming more conscious of our own *internal working models*, a phrase used by John Bowlby to indicate how a parent biologically entrains a child to fit into *this* environment of family and culture through the early attachment relationship.

In affect regulation, the etching of the attachment relationship into the brain and autonomic nervous system is done through accurate-enough *attunement* to the child's interior feeling world. This is how a child feels *known*. Of course, all of us were "etched" ourselves, so awareness of our own feelings is critical. Attunement to our feelings not only feeds our right hemisphere but, when we are with another, also can reorganize and heal hurts and misunderstandings from the past. The left hemisphere, however, should never be *left out* of the equation. The concepts held in our left brain have to be evaluated as to whether or not they serve one's true Self.

Dr. Placone's emphasis on building awareness of the present moment and weaving it into daily life while beginning to assess one's own family patterns is a right step toward a balanced right/left, body/mind. She clearly helps parents realistically evaluate their own lives and strengthen their "best self" through enhancing parent/child connectedness. In fact the very purpose of her book and training program is to enhance parent/child connectedness.

Dr. Placone appreciates the role of discipline and routine in child development and emotional regulation. Her book, *Mindful Parent Happy Child: A Guide to Raising Joyful and Resilient Children,* which focuses on increasing and strengthening mindfulness of the present moment, is a valuable addition to available parent/child resources.

What we need in our world and what continues to live on is the beauty of the heart. Children feed on their parents' happiness, protection, competence, and willingness to play and listen; in short, children want to feel they *belong* to those they love ... with all their heart. This requires all of us to be mindful of our own emotional health when we interact with those we love, especially an open-hearted child.

Dr. Placone's approach, which starts with mindfulness, and my approach, which starts with regulation, both work toward an integration of our body/mind that allows us to express the beauty of who we *truly* are. In this way, Dr. Placone and I are in complete agreement.

Ruth P. Newton, Ph.D.
San Diego, CA

Preface

In 1997 I was studying what parents, teachers, and mentors can do to help children avoid high-risk behaviors and effectively recover from difficult and painful experiences. In the course of my research, I discovered a longitudinal study concluding that a child's positive feelings of "parent-family connectedness" and "school connectedness" promote resiliency and significantly protect against high-risk behaviors, including drug and alcohol abuse, premature sexual initiation, and criminal activity.[1] When I read the words "parent-family connectedness," I felt as if I found the missing piece to a puzzle. Children who feel connected to their primary caretakers do better in their lives.

At the same time I was studying meditation practices and their potential contributions to the fields of human development and psychotherapy. A five-day stay at the Green

Gulch Farm Zen Center in Northern California deepened my own mindfulness meditation practice. In present moment awareness I began to find the promise of personal transformation. More than anything else this experience set me on a path to becoming a more compassionate and effective person.

Since then my research and clinical experience as a therapist have convinced me that:

1. ensuring the health and strength of the parent-child connection is—after physical safety—the highest priority for any parent or adult caregiver interested in growing happier and healthier children

2. a parent's own awareness of self and other is a primary ingredient in the establishment of a vital parent-child connection

These two insights led to the writing of this book on *Mindful Parenting*, that is, how to apply personal awareness in the service of raising more joyful and resilient children.

What Is Mindfulness?

The word "*mindfulness*" sparks an interesting reaction in some people: "Whoa! I'm not a Buddhist! I can't do this mindfulness thing! I don't meditate! Who has time?" If you have a similar response, take a deep breath, relax, and keep reading.

Mindfulness is very portable; it goes wherever you go. It can be practiced moment by moment as you shower, drive, watch TV, and—the primary reason for this book—build a healthier and happier relationship with the children in your life.

"Mindfulness" has been described in many different

ways and applied in many different contexts.[2] For now, it is enough to say that cultivating mindfulness involves the following:

- self-awareness
- observation and reflection
- description or identification of what is happening in the present moment
- a nonreactive acceptance of your internal experience
- an open, positive, and nonjudgmental approach to yourself and others

Such processes illustrate why "mindfulness" is often thought of not only as something you do, but also as a state or quality of being that is achieved through practices involving active reflection upon, and compassionate acceptance of, the self. Beyond this, the invitation to mindfulness is an invitation to live fully present in this moment and free of carelessness, corrosive judgments, or hurtful reactions. The following quote is a beautiful expression of mindfulness:

> *"Mindfulness doesn't tell us what to do, but it does give us a way to listen, a way to pay close attention to what we believe is important, and to expand our vision of what that might be in any situation, under any circumstances."*
> –Jon Kabat-Zinn

Mindful Parenting
As it turns out, the benefits of mindfulness extend beyond one's self. In this book you will explore and learn just how mindfulness can improve your parenting and cultivate a

Parental self-awareness, self-attunement, and self-organization are instrumental in developing a child's sense of self and capacities for living.

deeper connection with your child. How does this happen? As a parent becomes mindful, he or she becomes better at regulating thoughts, emotions, and physiological processes, and among other things, becomes more "self-attuned," empathic, and insightful. In effect, the parent cultivates a better relationship with him- or herself. What is so exciting and significant is that such *intrapersonal* changes not only alter the parent's brain function, they also have a corresponding *interpersonal* effect on the development of the children in his or her care. Parental self-awareness, self-attunement, and self-organization are instrumental in developing a child's sense of self and capacities for living.

Research continues to clarify how the quality of connectedness between parent and child plays a key role, not only in the development of a child's sense of safety or security,[3] but also in the formation of a child's regulation of thought, emotion, and physiology. It is now widely accepted that a child's attachment to a primary caregiver plays a major role in the organization of brain development[4] and functions related to attention.[5] Fundamental processes of growth and development (for example, how genes are expressed to enable us to survive and adapt) "are direct functions of the caregiving environment."[6]

Delving Deeper: The Roots of Mindfulness Practice

Practices of reflection, contemplation, meditation, and awareness have long been studied and developed within spiritually oriented communities, including those belonging to the world's many religious traditions. Hinduism, Buddhism, Taoism, Judaism, Christianity, Islam, and others have, in various times and places, generated practical methods for cultivating mindful states of consciousness.

For example:

- Hindu-oriented yogas, which for millennia have influenced the development of a wide variety of personal and relational characteristics—including physical strength, mastery of physiological processes, inner peace, knowledge, and devotion—continue to be practiced and refined today.
- Buddhist forms of meditation like *Vipassana* (in recent times also known as *Insight* or *Mindfulness* meditation) and *Zen* focus on the direct apprehension of experiences and reactions as they occur in this present moment of awareness. Buddhist practices also frequently prescribe different forms of sitting and walking that can give one, among other things, insight into the nature of reality and existence.
- Jewish Kabbalah invites mystical contemplation of sacred verses, words, letters, ciphers, and miraculous works that opens practitioners to a more profound understanding of, and relationship with, God and creation.
- Since the Middle Ages, Christians have approached mindfulness through practices of solitude, prayer, fasting, and contemplation within and beyond communal monasteries and cloistered communities.
- Sufism, a form of spirituality that emerged from Islam (but is not universally accepted by all strains of Muslim tradition), is generally concerned with direct experience of the Divine through specific dispositions and pietism to spark the development of a variety of new movements (e.g., Transcendentalism, Christian Science, New Thought, and Universalism) that were interested in the personal exploration and developmental processes of mind, perception, and reality.

As spiritual sages and teachers have long known, mindfulness practices increase self-knowledge, wisdom, compassion, and the capacity for living a more balanced life. They can open us to profound truths about the nature of reality: how everything around us and inside of us is impermanent, ever changing, and interconnected; how the more we try to avoid, suppress, deny, or struggle with the truth of "what is" in the present, the more we will suffer; how thoughtless reactivity, vengefulness, and resentment can amplify our individual and collective suffering.

The Contemporary Study of Mindfulness

The benefits of mindfulness practice have been long promoted by various spiritual communities and have been confirmed by scientific research. The evidence is clear: Mindfulness practice can stimulate personal growth and an increased sense of well-being. It can also assist significantly in recovery from addictions, the therapeutic management of personality disorders, and the improvement of mental and physical health.

Interest has grown worldwide in how best to understand and cultivate states and traits of consciousness that

1. promote personal and social well-being
2. transcend particular cultural and religious viewpoints. Leaders from a wide variety of philosophical, religious, and scientific communities have contributed to this growing movement.

While many important people deserve to be named here, I want to introduce you to three in particular:

Clinical Psychologist Jack Kornfield trained as a Buddhist monk in India, Thailand, and Burma. Since 1974 he has been teaching internationally and has written numerous books and articles on meditation practice. He works as a therapist and is the founder of Spirit Rock Meditation Center, where he currently lives, teaches, and considers himself an interpreter of Buddhist wisdom for the Western

As spiritual sages and teachers have long attested, mindfulness practices increase self-knowledge, wisdom, compassion, and the capacity for living a more balanced life.

world. He has observed that ongoing advances in science and technology make it necessary for us to develop a deeper inner understanding of ourselves. He also notes that our achievements in medicine, biology, physics, and neurology will not free us from warfare, racism, and environmental destruction. Such freedom requires a "parallel transformation of the heart" (2007). Kornfield teaches that human beings need to master compassion for each other and our world and that this can be accomplished through mindfulness practice.

Jon Kabat-Zinn is a researcher, writer, and meditation teacher who has pioneered clinical applications of mindfulness meditation. He, and other colleagues, are largely responsible for the surge of interest in mindfulness practice in contemporary medicine, psychology, business, and organizational development. He founded the renowned Stress Reduction Clinic at the University of Massachusetts Medical School. His eight-week Mindfulness-Based Stress Reduction (MBSR) program has helped thousands of people with physical and mental stress-related illnesses, everything from severe heart conditions to debilitating anxiety. His book, *Full Catastrophe Living* (1990), provides a non-religious approach to mindfulness and continues to be in great demand worldwide. MBSR has been researched cross-culturally and in a variety of fascinating settings, including hospitals and prisons. Continuing studies of MBSR have highlighted the beneficial effects of mindfulness practice on the brain, the immune system, processes of emotional regulation, recovery from surgical procedures, and many other areas of human experience and endeavor.

Jon, with his wife Myla, published the first book on the subject of mindful parenting, entitled *Everyday Blessings:*

The evidence is clear: Mindfulness practice can stimulate personal growth and an increased sense of well-being.

The Inner Work of Mindful Parenting (1997). This seminal work contributed to the development of a new field in psychology which is researching mindful parenting practices and their effects on both parents and children

Through research and clinical work in child psychiatry, interpersonal neurobiologist Dan Siegel has come to regard "mindfulness" as a critical ingredient in the relationships between children and their primary caregivers. After publishing a book entitled *Parenting from the Inside Out* (2003)—produced in collaboration with preschool director Mary Hartzell—Siegel was surprised at how frequently he was approached by people who assumed that he and Mary were teaching people to meditate, something he readily confesses he knew nothing about at that point in time.

"Mindfulness, in our view, was just the idea of being aware, of being conscientious, with kindness and care. We didn't actually teach parents to meditate, but rather taught them how to be reflective and aware of their children, and themselves, with curiosity, openness, acceptance, and love" (Siegel, 2007).

These questions about meditative practices led Siegel into conversation with the likes of Kornfield, Kabat-Zinn, his holiness the Dalai Lama, and many others interested in the promise of mindfulness. While it is important to honor the role religion has played in identifying and cultivating the phenomenon of mindfulness, Siegel's findings suggest that becoming more mindful in no way requires that one practice formal meditation or convert to a particular religious or spiritual viewpoint. He writes:

"How we focus attention helps directly shape the mind. When we develop a certain form of attention to our here-

As we consciously attend to strengthening such capacities within ourselves, we can improve the quality of the parent-child connection and positively influence the formation of the brains and central nervous systems of the children in our care.

and-now experiences and to the nature of our mind itself, we create a special form of awareness called mindfulness" (ibid.).

Drawing on research by Kabat-Zinn (2004) and findings from neuroscience, Siegel (2007, 2009, 2010) proposes nine different processes—all related to functions managed in the brain's middle prefrontal cortex—that can be strengthened through mindfulness practices and interventions:

- *bodily regulation* of basic physiological phenomena like heart rate, respiration, and gastrointestinal processes
- *attuned communication* with others in which our own internal states of thought and feeling "resonate" with the inner world of another allowing us to experience a "felt sense" of the other
- *emotional balance,* or the ability to establish equilibrium when triggered into states of arousal or when experiencing feelings of not being in control
- *response flexibility,* which is evident in the capacity to pause or withhold an immediate response
- *fear modulation,* or the capacity to inhibit fear-related reactions and move toward reestablishing a sense of calm
- *empathy,* or the capacity to see things from another's point of view
- *insight,* or the capacity to know ourselves in the present within the context of past circumstances and imagined future events
- *awareness,* which refers to how we think and behave relative to a greater social good

- *intuition*, or the capacity for processing information from the body and other nonverbal sources of experience

As we consciously attend to strengthening such capacities within ourselves, we can improve the quality of the parent-child connection and positively influence the formation of the brains and central nervous systems of the children in our care. The ways in which we parents, teachers, and mentors attend to our own mental processes—and the behaviors related to those processes—significantly influence how today's children will live and behave as tomorrow's adults.

If you are interested in strengthening the connection between you and your child, *Mindful Parent Happy Child* will help. As you perform the exercises in this book and adopt and build upon the principles and practices provided, you can cultivate the deeper self-awareness and self-understanding you will need to parent more mindfully. You can also discover the benefits and blessings that can come from being a mindful parent and optimize the likelihood that your child will grow up to be resilient and joyful and happier. It all starts with you.

How to Use this Book

This book is designed to be resourceful, versatile, and easy to use. It features different avenues for learning that include the following:

Wide margins for jotting down notes and marking important passages

Call-out boxes that give emphasis to a critical point or concept

"Did You Know?" boxes that summarize factual information

"Delving Deeper" sections that provide interesting background information

Embedded quotes to aid reflection and reinforce certain ideas

Exercises that allow you to draw on your own experience as you seek to become a more mindful parent

A "Quick Glance" at the end of each chapter that emphasizes salient points, thus making a quick review easier

A Workbook to help you consciously put your learning into practice

Personal and professional anecdotes to illustrate the principles and practices and their relevance to real-life situations

"Mindfulness is very
portable; it goes
wherever you go."

Chapter One
Begin with Yourself

*"Parents who are faced with the development of
children must constantly live up to a challenge.
They must develop with them."*
–Erik H. Erikson

While some couples have mapped out family planning for the birth of each child, others suddenly find themselves confronted with an untimely pregnancy. In any case, when the news arrives that a baby is on the way, it is normal for maternal and paternal instincts to take over and for preparations to begin. It is understandable and commendable that parents-to-be would become interested in the countless books, classes, and workshops offering guidance to parents on just about every topic related to parenting. (See resource section at www.mindfulparenthappychild.com)

It is not unusual for parents, new and experienced, to feel insecure about the work of parenting. After all, parenting is by far the most difficult job of all and the one that carries the most responsibility. It represents a commitment that is likely to last more than eighteen years. It requires nurturance and attention during every stage of the child's life. Whether caring for a helpless newborn or challenging interactions with an all-knowing, impulsive teen, parents are faced with new challenges every day.

As a parent you must understand that despite all of your self-education and preparation and despite the natural processes of bonding, there will likely be many moments when you will feel out of control or become reactive in your relationship with your child. As regretful and ashamed as you may feel after such experiences, this does not mean you are a horrible or incompetent parent. It means you are human.

Delving Deeper: Oxytocin, The Bonding Hormone

Though oxytocin has been touted in the popular press as the "love hormone" and though the mystique of a hormone that spreads beatific peace and love through the brain is seductive, in reality, there is evidence that in many people, its subjective effects are hard to perceive[1]. Furthermore, though oxytocin does increase trust[2] and generosity[3], improves eye contact[4], emotion recognition[5], and empathy[6], its effects are not found in every group of people studied[7], reports of its effects are not uniformly positive (it enhances envy and gloating[8]), and—thankfully—it does not make people blindly credulous[9].

That said, in the area of parenting, the study of oxytocin has been particularly illuminative, and it is clear from converging evidence from a variety of mam-

---

malian species[10,11,12] that oxytocin forms part of a portfolio of centrally-acting molecules that tether the ties that bind.

For example, aside from oxytocin's role in birth and breastfeeding, studies of parent-child dyads give strong evidence that oxytocin is involved in the biology of bonds. For example, oxytocin levels are related to mother's bonding (i.e. gaze, vocalizations, positive affect, affectionate touch) with her infant[13], affectionate contact in mothers and stimulatory contact in fathers varied with their oxytocin levels[14], and giving fathers oxytocin increased their playfulness with their infants[15]. Emphasizing the importance of congruent communication, sensitivity and tracking, parent-child synchrony (coordination of gaze, touch, and proximity) varied with both oxytocin and cortisol[16], a stress horomone influenced by oxytocin[17]. Finally, women with different variants in the oxytocin receptor gene have different bodily responses to infant crying[18], and oxytocin levels appear related to adult attachment and women's brain responses to their infants[19].

On the more sobering side, there is evidence that the central oxytocin system may be one of the stress-hormone systems which can be adversely impacted by early trauma[20]. That is, early relationships may actually permanently alter the activity of oxytocin genes in the brain, a kind of post-birth, experience-dependant genetic alteration called "epigenetic" changes[21,22]. Oxytocin is lower in the spinal fluid of women with abuse[23], its levels vary depending on presence of early abuse[24], and it improves attachment responses in adults with insecure attachment[25]. So aside from its potential as a therapeutic agent—a potential that is just beginning to be explored—the study of oxytocin underscores the importance of early experience in permanently sculpting the brain's stress and bonding systems[1].

This entry was generously contributed by Kai Macdonald, M.D. Voted as one of "San Diego's Top Doctors" by his peers in 2009 and 2010, Dr. Macdonald is a practitioner in Psychiatry and Family Practice, a faculty member at the University of California, San Diego, a researcher and author of numerous clinical trials.

The Benefits of Being a Mindful Parent

In our *Mindful Parent Happy Child* classes, we set out to help parents understand themselves better while they develop skills that encourage a healthy and lasting parent-child connection. Many who have worked on parenting mindfully testified to positive changes in the overall atmosphere or mood within their homes. Parents who were initially worried about how easily they were triggered into uncontrolled rage by something their children said or did have been able to "maintain calm in the middle of the storm." Other benefits reported are as follows:

- the *enjoyment* that can come from spending extra time and attention on yourself
- an *increased sense of closeness* with your children
- *feelings of confidence* that come when you successfully bypass potential power struggles with your child

Here are a few actual testimonials from parents:

"Mindful Parenting has helped me feel like a successful parent and left my children feeling loved and understood. What could be more fulfilling as a parent?"
–Julie

"This class has taught me to be aware of how I communicate with my children. This awareness has given more attention to the positive attributes, therefore creating a more balanced and loving relationship. Thank you for taking the time to help all children and parents."
–Maryha

"As a participant in the Mindful Parent Happy Child class, I was able to use what I learned to connect more deeply with myself and, in turn, more deeply with my children. Sharing experiences and concerns with other parents as we learned tools of mindfulness reassured me that I am constantly evolving as a parent and a person."
–Katy

The methods of mindful parenting are not a panacea, nor will they transform you or your relationship with your child overnight. Becoming a mindful parent requires consistent and concerted effort in the direction of a long-term goal. With such effort, you and your family can reap the rewards for years to come.

Now that you have some idea of the benefits of being a Mindful Parent, let's begin laying the foundation of the *Mindful Parent Happy Child* program.

How Do I Start?

Wherever you are, whatever you are doing, you can *begin* cultivating mindfulness by taking three simple steps:

1. Practice present-moment awareness of your thoughts, emotions, sensations, and surroundings.
2. Name or label what you become aware of.
3. Mentally "step outside" of your internal assumptions, judgments, and emotional reactions to people and circumstances and note how they help, limit, or oppress you.

Parents who were initially worried about how easily they were triggered into uncontrolled rage by something their children said or did have been able to "maintain calm in the middle of the storm."

You can begin to incorporate these practices into ordinary activities of daily living. For example, at times throughout your day you may choose to do the following:

⇒ Take mini-awareness breaks by stopping what you are doing; take a few deep breaths; pause and reflect on the people and circumstances in life for which you are grateful.

⇒ Pay attention to the thoughts, emotions, and sensations that arise as you do daily activities such as washing dishes, folding laundry, working in the garden, or performing other routine chores.

⇒ Envision those people, animals, and issues you are concerned about in life, and imagine directing thoughts and feelings of lovingkindness toward them.

⇒ Keep a journal in which you observe and note your inner and outer responses to life as it unfolds.

⇒ Take a walk in nature and consciously open your senses to the richness of the experience.

Starting with these simple mindfulness practices will help you start building a deeper and more positive connection with yourself and, ultimately, with the children in your life.

What if I Don't Like to Meditate?

Some people cultivate mindfulness in their daily lives through strictly prescribed methods of meditation or contemplation. Their practices can include extended periods of sitting or walking meditation. Some attend retreats that promote specific types of meditation, contemplation, or reflection.

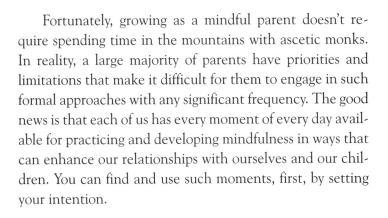

"Walking meditation is the one that everyone can do. There are those of us who find it difficult to practice sitting meditation, but almost everyone walks. And if you are in a wheelchair, you can do a rolling meditation"
–Thich Nhat Hanh

Fortunately, growing as a mindful parent doesn't require spending time in the mountains with ascetic monks. In reality, a large majority of parents have priorities and limitations that make it difficult for them to engage in such formal approaches with any significant frequency. The good news is that each of us has every moment of every day available for practicing and developing mindfulness in ways that can enhance our relationships with ourselves and our children. You can find and use such moments, first, by setting your intention.

Set Your Intention

Whatever your preferences in practice may be, as you work your way through this book, there are three key ideas I urge

Mindfulness is an invitation to live fully present in this moment—just as this moment is—without corrosive judgments or hurtful reactions.

you to keep in mind. Set your intention with the following affirmations:

1. *I can parent on purpose.* As I learn to pay attention to my own patterns and reactions of thought, emotion, and behavior, I'll become clearer about why I'm behaving in a particular way. I will see more clearly and be better able to decide whether or not a particular behavior is likely to promote a more secure connection with my child.

2. *Change is possible.* As I regularly work on developing self-awareness, self-understanding, and self-acceptance, I will expand my capacity for perceiving and responding more effectively to life and its demands. I will become more flexible and positively responsive in relation to myself and others.

3. A *healthier parent-child connection is my aim.* I am investing my time and energy to become a mindful parent in order to influence how my child grows and develops. Through mindfulness practice, I can deepen and maintain a parent-child connection that will provide the fertile ground my child needs to blossom and thrive.

Key Aspects of Mindfulness Practice

Now let's consider the following five key aspects of mindfulness practice in detail:

- self-awareness
- self-observation
- describing what is happening (in the present moment)

- nonreactivity (acceptance of your internal experience)
- nonjudgmental approach to yourself and others

Self-Awareness

In the bustle of everyday life, it is easy for parents to live largely on autopilot, unaware of how we might be neglecting ourselves and our children. Mindless living is evident in the following sorts of situations:

- eating when you're not hungry or overeating in an attempt to comfort yourself
- buying things you don't need
- missing a well-known turnoff or freeway exit close to your home
- shouting at your children in anger or responding to your child from feelings of guilt with little thought as to whether this is effective or appropriate

We all have occasions in life when we lose mental, emotional, and physiological balance. At such times, we may find ourselves boiling over with frustration. We can fail to notice our fatigue and how it contributes to increased irritability and loss of patience. We can become deluded, believing that we are caring well for ourselves and our children, simply because their favorite cereal is in the cupboard

> In the bustle of everyday life, it is easy for parents to live largely on autopilot, unaware of how we might be neglecting ourselves and our children.

"No matter how calmly you try to referee, parenting will eventually produce bizarre behavior, and I'm not talking about the kids."
–Bill Cosby

and the newest Super Mario Bros.' Wii™ game is loaded in the DVD player. Preventing these sorts of things from happening requires us to become more aware of *what we are doing and why we are doing it.*

As we take the time to become more aware of our personal patterns of thought, feeling, sensation, and behavior, we open ourselves to the possibility of gaining helpful insights that can facilitate better choices in our interactions with our children. As we purposefully deepen our self-awareness, we no longer have to be driven by habitual patterns of reactivity. Self-awareness is the platform of consciousness from which we can direct our mental attention to manage the characteristically automatic activity in the brain. Self-awareness allows our mind the opportunity to occupy the driver's seat, enabling the mind to steer the brain into new patterns of response and self-expression.

The Daily Benefits of Awareness

Deepening our awareness can benefit everyone in the family, including the family pets! For example, for some time I have insisted that our family dog get two walks and some playtime daily. At first, I couldn't explain why. I just knew it had to be done. It did not matter how busy and tired I was or what the weather was that day; I made sure Zeke got out for his recurring workouts. Over time I came to understand why I insisted on this ritual. I felt—without consciously realizing it—that chaos ensued when Zeke didn't get his regular walks and playtime: He paced around the house, pulled his cookies out of the pantry, ate ballpoint pens, and demolished my reading glasses.

On days when Zeke does get the activity he needs, he is more relaxed and satisfied, content to just lie around and

Self-awareness is the platform of consciousness from which we can direct our mental attention to manage the characteristically automatic activity in the brain.

be close to me and other members of the family. At such times he is happy, and so am I. Now this routine has more purpose, no matter what my mood is, and attending to Zeke comes more naturally. New practices have been incorporated and reinforced into our family's daily activities, resulting in an increased sense of balance within me, Zeke, and our home.

Undoubtedly you have a clear rationale for many of the things you do to keep your family running smoothly. Of course, this often involves much more than taking a dog on walks. For instance, you probably don't give your child candy before bedtime. Why? Through experience you know that sugar will "amp up" your child at a time when energies should be winding down, and you want to make it easy for your child to transition to dreamland. It's not hard to comprehend why withholding sweets at bedtime is a wise and reasonable thing to do. However, many of our other actions as parents are not as easy to explain or control.

"The wonderful gift of mindfulness is that we can stop ourselves and ask: What am I feeling? What is it like from my child's point of view? When you can do that, you often see things that you didn't let yourself see before because you were so caught up in the reactive mode, which is very limiting."
—Myla Kabat-Zinn

A more comprehensive self-awareness of *how you are*, *what you are doing*, and *why you are doing it* comes as you regularly pay attention to your own internal experiences and responses. Often even the briefest shifts in your attention will help you make positive adjustments in the lenses through which you look at yourself and the world around you. As you become more self-aware, you can discover essential insights into how you are engaging life. Such insights can lead you to make some intentional changes. This attention to yourself is a critical first step toward a high-quality connection with your child.

Self-Observation

As you develop lenses of self-awareness, you also create the necessary conditions for self-observation. You become an active watcher of your self and your own experiences from a state of mind that is more calm and nonreactive. Teachers of meditation have referred to this way of perceiving one's self, experiences, and activities in various ways—as the Witness, the Observing Self, or the Higher Mind. In my mindful parenting workshops, I simply refer to it as the *Observer*. The Observer is you observing you—your thoughts, feelings, sensations, and behaviors—in the present moment from a more objective perspective. Shifting your awareness to a standpoint of self-observation can provide you with helpful emotional distance and foster an open mental state wherein new and different thoughts and feelings can be entertained. This makes it possible for you to engage what's happening in *this* moment of life with less reactivity and more acceptance, curiosity, and gentleness.

Try this exercise: Imagine you are on the viewing deck of the Empire State Building. It is wintertime. When you look down, you see a swirl of colorful hats worn by ice skaters as they whirl around the rink at the Rockefeller Center. As you open your awareness to the grandeur of the view, you take in the famous Chrysler building and most of Manhattan. You also begin to notice an increasing number of

As you become more self-aware, you can discover essential insights into how you are engaging life. Such insights can lead you to make some intentional changes.

details: architectural features; clouds in the sky; miniature boats on the water; planes in the air; and taxis, cars, and buses on the streets far below. As my stepson Ian—a resident of New York City—describes it, you start to feel as if you are looking at *just about all of humankind.*"

From the top of the Empire State Building, you give yourself an angle of vision that opens you to perspectives and possibilities that are novel, intriguing, and inspiring. You notice many things from up high that you would be unable to experience while walking along the noisy, bustling, and sometimes overwhelmingly crowded city streets below. As the Observer on the observation deck you see everything from a completely different perspective. This vantage point may seem quite strange at first. It may even cause you to feel a bit weak in the knees, but that's okay. What is important is that you hang on to the railing and open yourself to what the sights have to teach you.

Strengthening your skills of self-observation does not mean you should walk around in a detached, unfeeling fashion or be perpetually insulated and isolated from the noisy, bustling, and crowded spaces of life or mind. The benefits of self-observation go beyond the insight and calm that can be experienced when you mentally step outside the customary flow of immediate experience.

As you practice moving between the Observer and the parts of yourself that act, interact, and react within the hubbub of daily life, you will ultimately help yourself:

- multiply your range of options for responding to yourself, family, and life circumstances in general
- shift your perspective more fluidly when you want to disrupt negative or unhelpful thoughts, expressions of emotion, or negative behavior

The Observer is you observing you—your thoughts, feelings, sensations, and behaviors—in the present moment from a more objective perspective.

When you have an *over-the-top* reaction to something—as if you became possessed and couldn't stop yourself—the Observer can help you get back into a balanced state of being. Practicing self-awareness as the Observer of your "self" (senses, body, thoughts, feelings, and interconnectedness) will increase your ability to maintain a healthy degree of mental and emotional balance and open you to different insights and avenues for action. It will help you become less reactive and more thoughtful.

Nowadays my Observer steps in when I'm stressed; she carries on a friendly internal dialogue with me that has to do with areas in which I am feeling out of control or crippled by harsh self-criticism. My Observer typically starts off with the word "Oh!" Then, in a singsong voice with a Midwestern accent (much like the character Barb from a *Ketchup Advisory Board* commercial on that classic public radio program *The Prairie Home Companion*), my Observing self will say something like the following:

"Oh, look. I am watching myself be harshly self-critical because I forgot to respond to an e-mail."

"Oh, look. Anger is rising in my chest as I look for my keys."

"Oh, look. My jaws are clenching as the person in front of me is writing a check in the cash-only line."

My Observer disrupts the ways in which I discount myself or others and engages my lack of self-acceptance with acceptance. She doesn't say any of the following:

"Pilar, if you weren't such a lazy person you wouldn't forget to respond to that e-mail."

When you have an over-the-top reaction to something—as if you become possessed and couldn't stop yourself—the Observer can help you get back into a balanced state.

"Pilar, if you weren't such a dolt you would place your keys in one place!"

"Pilar, I can't believe how impatient you are being; you still do this after all these years of mindfulness practice?

Consider the following challenging scene and how it relates to your own practices of self-awareness and observation:

> *After arriving home from a long, tiring day, your sweet child starts to burn off some excess energy by running around the kitchen table while squealing in an excited, high-pitched voice. Before you learned how to be the Observer of yourself, you might have reacted without thinking by yelling, "Stop!" or "Shut up!" in a tone of voice that might have been threatening, loud, or even more highly pitched than your child's. By itself, this incident would probably not represent a defining moment in your child's overall development, but while your immediate reactions may succeed in momentarily squelching your child's aggravating behavior, they will certainly fail to support the long-term results you want to have for your child and with your child.*

Standing on the self-observation deck

At the first sign of mindless reactivity, mentally move yourself to the "self-observation deck" and become the Observer of the situation. See yourself in the context of the present moment. Doing so can help you become aware of tiredness in your body, rapid and shallow breathing, or holding your breath. You may also notice a zillion different thoughts zipping in and out of your head or become aware that you are feeling exasperated or overloaded. As your child continues to run around squealing, the Observer can give you the internal space you need to be able to think of different possibilities, such as "Maybe this is exactly what he needs to do for a while." Such an insight may lead you to give yourself a break and to just sit on the floor while you allow him a few minutes of free expression before interceding to calm him down. Perhaps, as you take a little mental space, you will be able to realize that eventually he will tire himself out, which will make your intervention easier. You may identify how you can take care of yourself later; for example, you might go to bed a little earlier at night or hire a babysitter so that you can go out and experience some "adult time" with your spouse or a friend.

Moving to your "self-observation deck" can give you the mental space you need to think, attend to various aspects of yourself and your own needs, and consider the real demands of a situation *before* you react. With practice, such shifts in attention will help you *re-attune* to yourself and reestablish a sense of personal balance so that you can take better care of yourself and your child.

Describing What's Happening

As you shift your mental perspective to being the Observer, the benefits of awareness can be amplified by mentally noting, naming, and describing to yourself what you are observing.

Take a few slow, deep breaths (close your eyes if you like) and put yourself back into the scenario of the running,

At the first sign of mindless reactivity, mentally move yourself to the "observation deck" and become the Observer of the situation.

squealing child. Imagine that you are tired after a particularly long day, while your child is full of energy and noise. As the scene unfolds, imagine that, at a point in time of your choosing, you can press a button and freeze the action. Now, with the action stopped, describe what you are experiencing to yourself. Notice your reactions, which may be a mixture of thoughts, feelings, and body sensations.

- Pay attention to what you are experiencing right now. If you find your attention wandering to past or anticipated future events, gently bring it back to what is happening in the present moment.

- Describe the reactions you are observing: whether they are thoughts, emotions, sensations, or something else. For example, you might observe the following: "I feel angry." "I want to strike out." "I wish I could have more energy." "My feet want to run out the door and take me to Bermuda." "My child hates me." "This feels like fingernails on a chalkboard." "This is hopeless!"

- Note the qualities and details of your reactions. For example, you can ask yourself these questions: "What are my thoughts?" "Are they negative or judgmental?" "What am I feeling?" "Why do I have this tightening in my stomach? Is it connected to the present or something that happened earlier in the day?"

The practice of describing the present moment can take you, the parent, into different types of awareness. Taking a few seconds to describe the present moment can stir up feelings of *awe*—not necessarily the immense awe you might have experienced when your baby first called you

Mindfulness rouses the deeper parts of ourselves that get buried beneath the surface of everyday life.

mom or dad or your daughter walked across the stage at her sixth-grade graduation. But if you really pay attention, you can notice how describing what you are experiencing deepens your sense of what is special, intense, or important about this moment. Doing this can bring you calm and balance your connection with yourself and your experience.

Mindfulness rouses the deeper parts of ourselves that get buried beneath the surface of everyday life. If we become too hurried and distracted, we can lose touch with our children: the struggles they are having, the emotions they are feeling, or the important milestones they are passing as they are growing up. On the other hand, when we give ourselves a little time and space during the day to peel back the surface covers of life—through practices of awareness, observation, and description—we are more likely to enjoy and appreciate the many precious treasures to be discovered within ourselves and the children we are raising.

Nonreactivity

Mindfulness practice helps parents better regulate their entire system. Emotional self-regulation provides parents the ability to deliberately respond to their child rather than unconsciously react. Such reactivity in a parent can be frightening and disconcerting for a young child. A flood of fearful feelings creates a lonely and stressful environment that overwhelms the child's internal experience. Children are unable to process the *why* behind Mommy's screams or the *why* behind Daddy's fist shaking. In the mind of a child it feels personal, and in response the child can build defensive walls to self-protect, which creates a vast parent-child disconnect.

To a child, feeling disconnected from a parent or caretaker can be a very frightening experience, one in which security becomes an issue in the child's immediate world. Children react to this feeling of insecurity and isolation in a variety of ways, such as withdrawal or aggression. If parents are not prepared for this kind of response from their child, and if their own unconscious wounds become triggered, more distance can be created. In this type of situation, a parent cannot be attuned to or attend to their child's immediate need for emotional safety and comfort, for they are in the grip of their historical conditioning.

Reactivity flourishes in the absence of mindfulness. It interrupts and compromises your connection with yourself and others. As a parent, reducing your own reactivity translates into a more secure and stable connection with your child. In turn, he or she is more likely to grow up to be a secure and stable adult. When you turn your mind to observing and describing what is happening in the present moment—whether it be anger, hurt, boredom, hysteria, or panic—you are in a better position to gain a healthier perspective, maintain psychological equilibrium, and create a better balance in your connection with your child.

Mindfulness practice is the art of focused self-direction. It involves using our minds to direct our attention, our perception, our bodies, our breath, and even the structures of our brain. Being mindful helps us to regulate our emotions better, thereby allowing us to be more available to our children. When we develop the skill of nonreactivity, we are creating an environment of emotional safety and stability, which is the ultimate environment for healthy brain development.

Mindfulness practice develops the skills necessary to become nonreactive:

Reactivity

flourishes in

the absence of

mindfulness.

Nonreactivity
promotes good
feelings in the
home and
deepens the
parent-child
connection.

⇒ When turning focused attention to something basic, like breathing, the body slows down; this in turn lowers our stress level and increases relaxation.

⇒ By being the Observer of our thoughts and emotions, we can intervene earlier, before we become reactive and out-of-control.

⇒ As we observe ourselves in the moment, we move more into our internal world; this helps us gain greater insight, understanding, and compassion toward ourselves.

As a stepparent I know firsthand what it is like to have a strong reaction to something minor because of unconscious feelings and issues. I have heard numerous stories about parents having reactions that create disconnection and cause harm to their child's well-being. This is not what we as parents want to do, but how we were parented has embedded in us certain implicit memories, incidents we may have internalized and personalized far beyond our own parents' intentions.

Parenting is stressful. There are hundreds of issues and developmental stages to navigate: colicky babies, potty training, children who can't sleep, sibling rivalry, tantrums, first day of school, poor grades, isolating behavior, questionable friends, dating, driving, and leaving home. Many of these situations and stages can generate a whole raft of emotions in a parent. Think back for a moment. Do you remember how your parents handled challenging issues and important milestones as you were growing up? Do any of your reactions stem from your childhood experience?

Nonreactivity promotes good feelings in the home and deepens the parent-child connection. As you apply your awareness and learn to manage your emotions more effectively—anger, sadness, fear, guilt, shame, and frustration—you will be able to think with clarity before you behave, intervene before you react, and respond with increased attunement toward yourself and your child.

Delving Deeper: Your Brain on Alert

Fear-based responses begin with an outside stimulus that triggers a complex and usually automatic reaction in the value-recognizing[1] region of the brain called the "amygdala." When the amygdala detects a threat, it activates the adrenal-cortical system and the sympathetic nervous system. Many stress hormones—including adrenaline, norepinephrine, and cortisol—are released into the bloodstream, and nerve pathways are excited to prepare the body for survival in the face of a threat.

This physiological process is behind the pre-wired "fight, flight, or freeze" response[2]. Heart rate and blood pressure become elevated; pupils dilate to enhance vision; blood glucose levels increase; more blood is diverted to energize muscles; and breathing becomes rapid and shallow[3]. Less essential functions—such as digestion, attention to detail, and the immune system—are compromised. Capacities for relaxation and analysis can be partially or completely overtaken by aggressive impulses or the urge to flee and hide[1].

Such reactions, once experienced in times of distress or trauma, can become conditioned and lead to problems in personal and social functioning. Some people may also have a greater genetic vulnerability to anxiety than others, which would make them more susceptible to such conditioning[4].

The good news is, with regular and persistent use, practices and interventions related to mindfulness can disrupt and temper the largely automatic patterns of reactivity related to high-stress circumstances[5].

Nonjudgment

Philosophers, sages, psychologists, and leaders in politics and religion have had much to say over the millennia about *judgment*. For our purposes "judgment" has nothing to do with discernment or the positive skill of making wise observations and decisions. In this context it refers to a negative, counterproductive state of thought and emotion.

Generally, there seems to be some agreement that *being authentically happy* and *being judgmental* cannot easily inhabit the same mental space. A judgmental manner of being negates, oppresses, diminishes, discounts, and creates dramatic oppositions. When carried to an extreme, it can result in the dehumanization or destruction of people and entire civilizations.

Turn on the television and allow yourself to observe how judgment works and how pervasive it is in our society. People get paid handsomely to play on and excite this human tendency to judge. Advertisers have carefully studied how to sell eye shadow to teenage girls with low self-esteem, or convince some insecure guy to shore up his manhood with a Hummer. Unfortunately, strategic marketing that plays to a "better-than/less-than" mentality is highly effective.

Judgment runs rampant in the media. For example, you can readily find anchormen and anchorwomen using emotion-laden words like "attacked" and "lambasted" when they are reporting on conflicts and disagreements between political and social leaders. You can hear popular radio hosts condemning others in various ways, calling them "stupid," "arrogant," "socialist," "fascist," and so on. Such disparagement negatively influences our minds and hearts and nurses seeds of hatred, distrust, and intolerance. We

Unfortunately, strategic marketing that plays to a "better-than/less-than" mentality is highly effective.

become competitors and opponents instead of sharing, caring neighbors. Is this what we want to be teaching the next generation?

Within our families we can observe the sinister effects of judgment (around the theme of "better than" or "less than") in our conversations. Here are some examples:

"Are you kidding? I won't let my kids wear anything but designer clothes."

"Those damn [insert a category of people of your choosing] are destroying our country! They should all be taken out and shot!"

"Anyone who believes in God is just plain stupid," or conversely, "Anyone who doesn't believe in God is a sinner and is going to burn in hell for all eternity."

Such illustrations are not overblown; I have heard some version of each of these more than once. Unfortunately, if we are exposed to this kind of judgment, so are our children. Children naturally pick up and absorb such messages from home and school. They readily internalize and integrate them into how they think and feel about themselves and others. Such messages can instill a feeling in a child that she or he is unworthy or unlovable. They encourage patterns of harsh criticism toward self and others. They also tend to fuel a corresponding fear of being judged and criticized by others.

Children who are steeped in such messages and lack strong and healthy connections with their parents and significant caregivers are at a significantly higher risk of becoming bullies or victims, insecure or entitled, isolated or gang members, anorexic or addicted. They will be more prone to seek the approval of a person they view as *better than* themselves, and this can take them down some very dark and dangerous roads.

> *"Everything that irritates us about others can lead us to an understanding of ourselves."*
> –Carl Jung

Like poisoned arrows, judgments that discount, disqualify, or diminish oneself or others can have a devastating impact on their target. Often our arrows are aimed directly at ourselves, injecting harsh self-criticism that negates and destroys healthy self-regard. The poison can then spread like a virus from interaction to interaction. Without an antidote or effective interventions within ourselves and our relationships, many of us will eventually succumb to the pandemic.

Mother Teresa of Calcutta said: *"If you judge people, you have no time to love them."* Her wise words get to the heart of the matter. If our minds are filled with judgmental thoughts, we have no room for thoughts of lovingkindness.

As long as we mindlessly judge ourselves and others, our growth as people and as parents is apt to be stunted or delayed. From the standpoint of mindful awareness and self-observation, we can learn to apprehend and neutralize our judgments without taking on the role of judge and jury of ourselves or our experience. We can put ourselves in a better position to cultivate the conscious space necessary for healing and transform our internal experience into something where, ultimately, *there is no negative judgment.*

Developing a nonjudgmental approach to living can

Developing a nonjudgmental approach to living can be helped by inviting compassion in toward ourselves and others. We can, with intentional practice, replace judgment with compassion.

be helped by inviting in compassion toward ourselves and others. We can, with intentional practice, replace judgment with compassion.

A few years ago, I had an opportunity to work with Jamie, a 30-year-old mother of a two-year-old boy. In our first session I learned that Jamie grew up in a family and subculture that promoted and inculcated in her a "better-than/less-than" attitude. During the visit Jamie offered a comment about how people can never change. I inquired what she meant by that, and she matter-of-factly responded, *"In general, people are either conditioned to be good or bad. Sometimes they are able to change their behavior, but they can never really change themselves."*

As she said this, I became immediately aware of my own judgmental reaction to her point of view. By being the *Observer* of these judging thoughts, I self-intervened, interrupting my own inclination to contradict or correct her. Instead, I kept listening. Jamie's point of view, after all, was what she had summed up about the world around her, and more than likely, her style of thinking in some way mirrored that of her primary caretakers.

I wanted Jamie to feel safe so she could share her ideas without fear of being judged. I intentionally provided a hospitable environment where Jamie could freely express her opinions. Removing my initial judgment gave way to empathy and compassion for Jamie, thereby enabling me to provide an accepting and trusting relationship. Along the way, I gave her some encouragement and asked her some questions that helped her explore her thinking further.

Though my initial reactive impulse was to change her outlook by arguing with her, I was able to choose a softer approach which exposed her to a less "black and white" world. By maintaining an environment of openness and acceptance, I invited Jamie into a safe space where she could engage in deeper, less judgmental self-examination and more likely arrive at an optimistic and accepting conclusions.

Mindful parents take time to identify the ways they were taught to judge themselves by their family members, social groups, and other important influences in their background. Then they go on to explore which of these patterns of judgment they have carried into their parenting and how they have been transmitting them to their children. Understandably, this latter step can be excruciating for any parent. Who wants to examine the judgments they have toward their own children?

As parents in the *Mindful Parent Happy Child* program learn to observe their judgments of themselves and their children mindfully, they open themselves to healing and eradicating the negativity and reactivity that arises from judgment. Through a trusting connection with their instructor and other group members, they can discover a deeper understanding of how they are, what they do, and why they do it. They can begin to replace judgment with compassion.

How Mindfulness Builds the Parent-Child Connection

Only when we have a depth of self-understanding that comes from connecting well with ourselves can we connect well with our children. On the surface this level of understanding may appear fairly easy to accomplish, but—as any dedicated parent, teacher, or mentor can tell you—it can

> Mindful parents take time to identify the ways they were taught to judge themselves by their family members, social groups, and other important influences in their background.

be fraught with challenges.

As you purposefully and consistently practice mindfulness, you will progressively expose automatic patterns of experience, thought, feeling, and reaction that shape how you live and express yourself. You'll become more conscious of the core beliefs, attitudes, prejudices, coping styles, and myriad patterns of thought and emotion you have either inherited from your family of origin or somehow developed in the course of your own life experience.

Paying mindful attention to yourself and your own reactions can help you understand "how" you are at this point in time—what you do, why you are doing it, and more. When you consistently practice paying attention, on purpose, to what is happening inside you right now—with an attitude of acceptance and nonjudgment—you begin to dig at the roots of less healthy mental and emotional states and the negative behaviors that are generated by them. You disrupt their continued reinforcement and growth, and you are laying the necessary groundwork for becoming more connected with yourself.

Delving Deeper: You Can Change Your Brain

The brain is a complex organ comprised of interconnected systems and structures, including approximately 100 billion interconnected nerve cells called *neurons*. Before 1998 it was commonly believed that the number of neurons and neuronal connections in the adult brain were fixed and unchanging and that the structures and systems of the brain were, for the most part, genetically predetermined and incapable of significant reorganization or change[1].

Within the past decade many of our assumptions about the brain and how it works have been challenged. While the brain can be severely compromised by disease or injury, it is capable of adaptation and healing. Its structures and pro-

---

cesses can continue to change and grow throughout our lifetimes. In response to physical, psychological, and social stimulation, neurons can increase in number, new neural pathways can develop, and genes can be activated or deactivated. A great deal of research is being done in an effort to understand the brain's potential for making such changes.

Science has clearly established that mindfulness-based practices alter brain function[2]. Mindfulness-based stress reduction can lower emotional reactivity and rumination[3], reduce symptoms of depression and anxiety[4], improve the function of the immune system[5], and strengthen attentional control[6]. Mindfulness training may even "protect against functional impairments associated with high-stress" work environments[7]. Researchers in China[8] found that twenty minutes of integrative body-mind training over five days yielded observable and measurable improvement in attentional control and the regulation of basic autonomic functions like respiration and heart rate.

A child needs

from caring adults

a sense of being

known, of being

understood—

really seen and

heard.

Over time, with mindfulness practice you can realize a greater sense of inner calm, self-attunement, and self-acceptance. Day-by-day, moment-by-moment, the old habits will gradually give way to feeling more comfortable and controlled in your internal world. You'll reduce your automatic emotional reactions and become more balanced and deliberate, more gentle and understanding with yourself and in your interactions with others.

Such self-awareness has nothing to do with "navel-gazing" or self-centered preoccupation. As we have seen, its value extends far beyond the self. A secure relationship with a primary caregiver(s) can either help or hinder a child's:

- development of optimism and resiliency

- ability to recognize and choose not to engage in high-risk behaviors
- success in life

A child's brain and central nervous system support and express his or her patterns of thinking, feeling, and responding to life. These patterns are significantly shaped in the relationship that has been established with his or her parent figures. A child needs from caring adults a sense of being known, of being understood—really seen and heard. In a secure and stable relationship in which they feel accepted, children are better able to develop skills necessary for coping and adapting with life's many challenges. In short, the development of more secure and stable children requires a secure and stable connection with the parents and key adults in their lives. And such a connection is rooted in the quality of a parent's subjective connection to him- or herself. It is a resource that can be developed through some sort of mindfulness practice.

Did You Know

People who practiced "lovingkindness meditation"—with the intention of experiencing positive emotions during meditation and in life in general—saw an increase in life satisfaction and social support and a decrease in symptoms of depression and illness.

Quick Glance: Chapter One

On Mindful Parenting

⇒ As it turns out, the benefits of mindfulness extend beyond one's self. In this book, you will be exploring and learning just how mindfulness can help you improve as a parent. How does this happen? As a parent becomes mindful, he or she becomes better at regulating thoughts, emotions, and physiological processes; and among other things, he or she becomes more "self-attuned;" empathic, and insightful. Some benefits of mindfulness are:

- the *enjoyment* that comes from spending extra time and attention on yourself
- an *increased sense of closeness* with your children
- *feelings of confidence* that come when you successfully bypass potential power struggles with your child

How to Start: Three Steps

1. Practice present-moment awareness and observation of yourself and your experience.
2. Name or label what you become aware of.
3. Mentally "step outside" of your internal assumptions, judgments, and emotional reactions to people and circumstances, and note how they help, limit, or oppress you.

And . . .

Incorporate these practices into the ordinary and often mundane activities of daily living. For example, at times throughout your day you may choose to do the following:

⇒ Take mini-awareness breaks by stopping what you are doing. Take a few deep breaths; pause and reflect on the people and circumstances in life for which you are grateful.

⇒ Pay attention to the thoughts, emotions, and sensations that arise as you do daily activities such as washing dishes, folding laundry, working in the garden, or performing other mundane chores.

⇒ Envision those people, animals, and issues you are concerned about in life, and imagine directing thoughts and feelings of lovingkindness toward them.

⇒ Keep a journal in which you observe and note your inner and outer responses to life as it unfolds.

⇒ Take a walk in nature and consciously open your senses to the richness of the experience.

Set your intention
- *I can parent on purpose.*
- *Change is possible.*
- *A healthier parent-child connection is my aim.*

Key Aspects of Mindfulness Practice
- self-awareness
- self-observation
- describing what is happening (in the present moment)
- nonreactivity (acceptance of your internal experience)
- nonjudgmental approach to yourself and others

How Mindfulness Builds the Parent-Child Connection
⇒ As you purposefully and consistently practice mindfulness, you will progressively expose those automatic patterns of experience, thought, feeling, and reaction that shape how you live and express yourself. You'll become more conscious of the core beliefs, attitudes, prejudices, coping

styles, and myriad patterns of thought and emotion you inherited from your family of origin or developed through your own life experience.

⇒ Paying mindful attention to yourself and your own reactions can help you understand "how" you are at this point in time, what you do, why you are doing it, and more. When you consistently practice paying attention, on purpose, to what is happening inside you right now—with an attitude of acceptance and nonjudgment—you begin to dig at the roots of less healthy mental and emotional states and the negative behaviors generated by them.

⇒ A child's brain and central nervous system support and express his or her patterns of thinking, feeling, and responding to life. These patterns are significantly shaped in the relationship that has been established with his or her parent figures. A child needs from caring adults a sense of being known, of being understood—deeply seen and heard.

⇒ In short, the development of more secure and stable children requires a secure and stable connection with the parents and key adults in their lives. And such a connection is rooted in the quality of a parent's subjective connection to him- or herself.

"Become the observer of

the situation."

Chapter Two
Choosing Your Family Heirlooms

Parenthood is the passing of a baton, followed by a lifelong disagreement as to who dropped it.
–Robert Brault

Parenting practices are comparable to family heirlooms that are passed down from one generation to the next. Some are beautiful treasures while others are outmoded or downright ugly.

In the course of being a stepparent, I discovered firsthand how the brain can be trained through the intentional use of the mind to sort through and either keep or discard my own inherited parenting practices.

When I became a stepmom, I quickly realized that my brain had been "prewired" in my childhood in ways that had not prepared me for my current situation. My new stepchildren, Ian and Claire, would frequently do things that made little sense to me, and, in response, I would become emotionally prickly. At such times, sarcastic questions swarmed in my head, such as *"Why is that backpack and its contents spread all over my favorite chair?"* or *"How many empty water bottles does it take to cover a 9 by 11 bedroom floor?"* or *"Does my blow-dryer have feet?"*

The sarcasm came from negative judgments that set my "right way" of perceiving and doing things against their "wrong way" of being and behaving. After several of these judgmental moments, I eventually realized that I was reacting and behaving based on what *my parents* had modeled and taught me. Not that my parents' ways were wrong, but they were frequently different from the behaviors I was witnessing as a stepparent. My older siblings and I never would have been allowed to leave our backpacks and personal belongings lying around the house, especially in my dad's reading chair! During my early stepmom days, my brain was being challenged to develop new neural pathways, different from those that had served me so well during my years as a child and single adult.

All parents and primary caretakers face the same challenge: Parents have been wired to parent as they were parented. In our childhood, our brains developed particular neural pathways, a process in which synaptic firing communicated and built connections among neurons in different regions of our brains. Such structures have a direct influence on the attachment bond we have with our child, and, in turn, these attachment bonds drive the development and integration of neural pathways in the brains and nervous systems of the children in our care.

> *"If there is anything we wish to change in a child, we should first examine it and see if it is something that could better be changed within ourselves."*
> –Carl Jung

While growing up, I had been conditioned (or wired) to expect that, if I left my backpack and possessions lying around the house, I would get in trouble. This became an embedded belief in the area of my memory called *implicit memory*. Implicit memory is encoded in us beginning with our first year of life, without any involvement of conscious awareness. This is why I had negative reactions to my stepchildren if they did something that was opposite of my encoded belief of the way things *should* be. Until I was able to identify the unconscious belief, or the embedded "should," I was unable to operate as the stepparent I consciously desired to be. I soon learned I had some rewiring to do if I wanted them to develop a healthy bond with me.

Delving Deeper: Highlighting Implicit Memory

Implicit memory, the form of memory available in our first twelve to eighteen months, is a crucial function of the amgydala—the initial meaning-making center of the brain. Implicit memory is where our earliest encoding takes place. If you are reacting and you don't know why, this likely means your implicit memory has been triggered by something familiar—positive or negative—from your past. Implicit memory, just one of the numerous functions in the amygdala, contains elements of emotional experiences, perceptions, behavioral responses, bodily sensations, and images. Repetition of these experiences form into "mental models" [1] that are processed through the amygdala where we then form our own conclusions about how life works and where we fit in. With age these mental models, if left unconscious, can direct our decisions, behaviors, and reactions regardless of our most earnest desires.

It is also important to realize that responses rooted in implicit memory often overlook the distinction between past and present. What you are experiencing in the present and your reaction to it—emotionally, physically, sensationally— might very well have more to do with some past experience [2].

As a novice stepparent, I wanted to earn Claire's and Ian's trust and be close with them. But I experienced an internal conflict between what I wanted ideally and the negative thoughts and feelings within me that were triggered by their different ways of being and behaving. In the course of my own mindfulness practice, I came to see clearly how the tension I felt toward Ian and Claire had very little to do with them. It really began with my own internal states of mind and emotion.

By every objective measure, Ian and Claire were (and are) outstanding young people: bright, caring, easygoing, and adaptable. They displayed secure attachment with their dad, themselves, and other people. They were fun, interesting, communicative, flexible, confident, and happy. They were open, and they accepted me into their lives with grace and ease. On the surface, and as far as they were concerned, all was good. Why then was I under siege mentally and emotionally? To put it simply, the wiring in my brain was preventing me from being the parent I wanted to be. I needed to do some rewiring so that I could live peacefully in my new situation. Mindful awareness helped me see where I needed to change old neural pathways.

When I went from being single and living alone to having an instant family, I was fortunate to have already incorporated mindfulness practice into my life; in fact, I had nearly completed my dissertation on Mindful Parenting. The *Mindful Parent Happy Child* model that I used then is the same process I use today when my internal world and behavior are incongruent with my intentions. I had to do my own personal growth work to be a mindful stepparent, and I am convinced this is why I have developed such a strong and meaningful connection with Ian and Claire, and subsequently with their spouses.

"To know how one is conditioned is the first step to freedom . . .
To be aware is not to be superficially conscious, but to go into
full depth of consciousness so as not to leave undiscovered one's
unconscious reactions."
–J. Krishnamurti

We can also find ourselves parenting in opposition to what was modeled for us as we were growing up. Whatever the case, unsupportive or hurtful parenting usually comes from a state of mindlessness and reactivity. Mindful parents bring unexamined parenting behaviors to consciousness. Developing a more purposeful way of parenting involves becoming more aware of what we inherited. A good way to begin this process is to consider your answers to the question, "What legacy do I want to pass on to my child?"

Those who specialize in studying and treating family systems have long known that the psychological wounds and dysfunctions we carry into our adult lives and relationships have often been passed down to us from generations past. Very few parents consciously want to pass on such problems to their children. Most simply wish to love and cherish them and provide them with the best opportunities possible. They want them to grow up to be good citizens and self-sufficient adults. They help their children complete their educations, make friends, and generate a reliable moral compass to guide them through life.

Unfortunately, good wishes are often not enough to overcome the powerful *multigenerational transmission process* at work in family life (Bowen, 1978; Kerr, 2005) whereby negative patterns of thought, emotion, and behavior are transferred from parent to child.

Wounds from childhood can lie dormant in our unconscious until we have a child of our own (Miller, 1979). This problem is compounded by the fact that parents frequently fail to learn and to integrate the skills necessary for raising psychologically and socially healthy children.

Without a conscious, ongoing effort to identify and heal these wounds—and alter the patterns of behavior related to them—we risk unintentionally transmitting them to children. Mindfulness practice facilitates the levels of consciousness necessary to interrupt this process and makes it possible for you to choose a legacy different from the one you inherited, one you will be proud to pass on to future generations.

As you become a mindful parent, you will become better prepared to reduce, if not entirely extinguish, the hurtful and potentially harmful aspects of your own social in-

Developing a more purposeful way of parenting involves becoming more aware of what we inherited.

heritance so that you can raise a healthier, happier family of your own.

Family Health Begins Here and Now

A healthy family is a happy family. Sounds reasonable, right? But you may be asking, *"What are some markers I can use to assess whether my family is on the healthy track?"*

Family health is related to how well:
⇒ parents consciously address their own psychological/relational wounds and dysfunctional patterns in order to prevent them from being passed down to the next generation

⇒ members of the family use rational thought, constructive behaviors, and effective communication to enhance baseline levels of trust and mutuality within the family

⇒ the family works together to create a relational environment that generates, supports, and reinforces positive emotional experiences, especially in the earlier stages of childhood development

Stop for a moment and reflect on how well you think your family is doing in these three areas. Write a few notes in the margins or in a journal answering this question: Which of these areas do I need to work on, and which of those should become a priority?

Mindfulness practice facilitates the levels of consciousness necessary to interrupt this process, and makes it possible for you to choose a legacy different from the one you inherited, one you will be proud to pass on to future generations.

Examining Your Family Background

The values, beliefs, and styles of communication and responsiveness you inherited may or may not be your ideal. Yet like your parents, you are probably doing the best you can with what was handed down to you. (Of course, there are exceptions, and if you come from a history of abuse, addiction, or neglect, you may have a different story to tell.) If possible, entertain the possibility that your parents did the best they could. Sometimes this in itself can help you leave behind the failings of your own parents and move forward in your growth and development as a parent.

Now use the following questions to help you reflect upon your personal experience growing up:

1. How did your parent(s) or caregiver(s) successfully resolve conflicts and otherwise communicate in positive and constructive ways?
2. Did your family of origin provide an environment in which you felt safe and could express yourself without fear?
3. What prevailing moods and behaviors were indications of a lack of health and happiness?

You can also learn more about the "heirlooms" you inherited by spending a day or two paying close attention to how you interact with your children from moment to moment. Notice which patterns of interaction and reaction are similar to those you experienced in your family of origin. Take note of the following:

- the ways you show love and affection to your children
- the methods you use for applying discipline

If possible, entertain the possibility that your parents did the best they could.

- your reactions to tantrums, moodiness, or disrespect

When and if you discover any unresolved wounds your parents passed on to you, contemplate their impact on your child rearing and on how you would like their growing-up experience to be different.

How to Rewrite Your Story

Understanding who you are in your role as parent starts with taking an honest look at what is within you and where it came from. As you proceed with this task, you can take intentional steps toward a deeper self-understanding, and you can edit and even rewrite your life story. You can decide the ways of being and behaving you want to keep and those you want to leave behind. For example, if you commonly experienced harsh teasing or felt put down or shamed as a child, you can *choose* not to pass on this relational pattern to your own children. In becoming more aware of such patterns and choosing to change them, you may be surprised at how you can discover new ways of seeing and loving yourself that were formerly unavailable to you.

"Those who do not have the power over the story that dominates their lives, the power to retell it, rethink it, deconstruct it, joke about it, and change as times change, truly are powerless because they cannot think new thoughts."
–Salman Rushdie

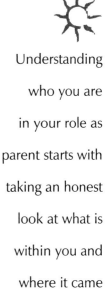

Understanding who you are in your role as parent starts with taking an honest look at what is within you and where it came from.

Roots and Branches: Building Your Genogram

As a family therapist I explore these kinds of questions with my clients by creating a *genogram*—a kind of family tree diagram that covers four or more generations. As the genogram is being drawn, my clients often experience surprise at the difference it makes to "see" the family story visually depicted. As connections and patterns of thought, emotion, and behavior that have been passed on from generation to generation become clearer, clients often gain helpful insights into themselves and their family members.

A warning is appropriate here. Drawing a genogram can bring up painful memories and emotions. It can confirm or challenge your customary perceptions about your family and yourself, and it can stimulate a variety of feelings—like anger, sadness, empathy, or compassion—toward yourself and family members. As awareness increases and patterns of connection become more conscious, such realizations can represent an important step toward changing your family legacy.

"A man can't make a place for himself in the sun if he keeps taking refuge under the family tree."
–Helen Keller

Now give yourself some time to build your own genogram. You'll become more familiar with the story you've been living until now, and you'll start to become aware of inherited patterns that you want to change.

Below is a list of twenty-one questions related to your family of origin. They should take about fifteen minutes to answer. In the workbook section of this book you will have the opportunity to come back to these questions. Write your answers in the extra space after each question. Take breaks as needed. Some questions may bring up memories, feelings, and new, unexamined realizations.

Note: *Some questions may not apply to you and the circumstances of your family; feel free to pass over them.*

1. Did one or both parents raise you, or were you adopted or raised by another family member? Explain.

2. Were there other significant caretakers in your life within or outside your family? (Use adjectives to describe their personalities and behaviors.)

3. How would you describe your parents' relationship?

4. If your parents separated or divorced, how would you describe its impact on you and the rest of your family?

5. Did either of your parents die before you left home?

6. Did you have a stepparent? If so, describe your relationship with him or her.

7. How did your mom show you that she loved you?

8. How did your dad show you that he loved you?

9. Did either or both of your parents have strong religious beliefs? If so, what kind of influence did this have on you?

10. Did you have favorite relatives? What made them special to you?

11. Did your parents show favoritism toward any of their children? If so, what was the impact on you?

12. Did you come from a family with clear and strict rules or loose, relaxed standards?

13. Was there any prejudice or discrimination in or against your family related to race, religion, sexual orientation, or other?

14. How was punishment or discipline administered?

15. How were feelings like sadness, fear, and anger handled?

16. Did you feel comfortable talking with your parent(s)?

17. How were sex and sexuality expressed and discussed in your family?

18. What addictions are evident in your immediate and extended family members (e.g., food, alcohol, drugs, work, and so on)?

19. Was there any emotional abuse, physical abuse, sexual abuse, or neglect?

20. Was there any long-term illness or trauma experienced by a parent or sibling?

21. Were there any other significant events or circumstances that deserve attention?

Now, take a few minutes to reflect on your responses to the foregoing questions. Write down your answers to the following questions:

1. Did this exercise bring forward new information, or are you seeing something differently than before?

2. Which questions were the hardest to answer? Why?

3. Do you see any patterns passed down to you that you want to keep and pass on to your children? What are they?

4. Do you see any patterns that you are passing down that you do not want to hand on to your children or that you want to alter in some way? What are they?

A Few Suggestions to Help You Along

Families are systems. Some are like well-oiled machines that occasionally need an adjustment here or there. Others could use a complete overhaul. Whatever the case in your family, as you sort through family heirlooms and begin to develop a more intentional sense of the legacy you want to leave to your children and grandchildren, you will do well to pace yourself. This is not something that can be accomplished in just a few days.

As you create a more complete picture of your family of origin, don't let your own opinions and feelings keep you from making an honest assessment of the legacy passed down to you. For example, if any of your forebears were criminals, members of a religious cult, considered sexual deviants, suffered from mental disorders, or were part of a racial group or socioeconomic class different from those with which you now identify, don't leave this information out of your genogram. With that said, it is also equally important to not get lost in being a victim of your childhood, as this can lead to unhealthy and destructive patterns. In his book "Hand-Me-Down-Blues," Dr. Michael Yapko states:

Coming to terms with what it means to have the choice about how you want to live from now on, and how you want to reshape your family's way of doing things it may not do very well right now, is the hallmark of maturity. Forever blaming others in your past for your problems and getting lost in the illusion that there's nothing you can do about the harm you think they caused you is a formula for failure. Take control and start doing something different, even if it is just a little bit different, today.
—M. Yapko, 1999

Remember, as you work at becoming a mindful parent, you can shed those heirlooms you don't want to pass on—including any skeletons in the family closet. In the final analysis, children need one thing more than anything else to maximize their chances of growing up to be well-adjusted and happy adults: They need you to be the best YOU you can be.

Quick Glance: Chapter Two

Inspired to Rewire

When I became a stepmom, I quickly realized that my brain had been "prewired" in my childhood in ways that had not prepared me for the current demands of parenting.

We can also find ourselves parenting in opposition to what was modeled for us as we were growing up. Whatever the case, unsupportive or hurtful parenting usually comes from a state of mindlessness and reactivity. As a mindful parent, you bring unexamined parenting behaviors to consciousness.

Those who specialize in studying and treating family systems have long known that the psychological wounds and dysfunctions we carry into our adult lives and relationships have often been passed down to us from generations past.

Without a conscious, ongoing effort to identify and heal these wounds—and alter the patterns of behavior related to them—we might unintentionally transmit them to children. Mindfulness practice facilitates the levels of consciousness necessary to interrupt this process and makes it possible for you to choose a legacy different from the one you inherited, one you will be proud to pass on to future generations.

Family Health Begins Here and Now

Family health is related to how well:

⇒ parents consciously address their own psychological/relational wounds and dysfunctional patterns in order to prevent them from being passed down to the next generation

⇒ members of the family use rational thought, constructive behaviors, and effective communication to enhance baseline levels of trust and mutuality within the family

⇒ the family works together to create a relational environment that generates, supports, and reinforces positive emotional experiences, especially in the earlier stages of childhood development

How to Rewrite Your Story

You can also learn more about the "heirlooms" you inherited by spending a day or two paying close attention to how you interact with your children from moment to moment. Notice which patterns of interaction and reaction are similar to those you experienced in your family of origin.

Understanding who you are in your role as parent starts with taking an honest look at what is within you and where it came from.

You can decide the ways of being and behaving you want to keep and those you want to leave behind. For example, if you commonly experienced harsh teasing or felt put down or shamed as a child, you can *choose* not to pass on this relational pattern to your own children.

"Learn how to plot, sow, and grow a thriving and bountiful family garden."

Chapter Three
Three Principles of Mindful Parenting

*"One wonderful seed is mindfulness . . . use every opportunity
to touch that seed and help it to manifest on the upper
level of your consciousness."*
–Thich Nhat Hanh

P arents are like gardeners, tending the children in
their care. We possess a variety of seeds that can
be sown within ourselves and in others, regardless
of whether they are seeds of love, hate, joy, fear,
generosity, or greed. If we want to raise a loving child, we
need to plant and tend the seeds that grow love.

Who we are now, as adults and parents, is in large part
a result of how the seeds within us were tended and watered
by our own parents and caregivers. As adults we are faced
with the task of taking over and becoming the responsible
caretakers of our own gardens. This requires that we reg-

ularly take a step back and observe for ourselves what is thriving and blossoming and what is withering or dying on the vine. Mindful parents take care to identify which plants could use more water or sunshine or fertilizer and which could use less. And rather than allow unwanted weeds to establish themselves and overtake our gardens, we make intentional choices about what is allowed to keep growing and what needs to be uprooted and tossed into the compost bin.

In making sense of our own inner gardens, we learn better how to plot, sow, and grow a thriving and bountiful family garden. As we decide which seeds we will nurture within ourselves, we are preparing the ground for similar growth in our children. Ultimately, it is through increased self-understanding, self-acceptance, and self-care that we will enable our children to cultivate a world in which people take better care of themselves and each other. Through our own individual efforts to live mindfully, we can adopt new ways of being, new ways of knowing, and new levels of compassion toward our children, our communities, and ourselves.

By incorporating and living *The Three Principle of Mindful Parenting*, you can become a master gardener. Along with other practitioners, you will be helping to grow a new and healthier world community, one family at a time.

The Three Principles

1. All adults are parents.
2. Parent-child connectedness grows happy children.
3. Mindful Parenting is a life practice.

> As we decide which seeds we will nurture within ourselves, we are preparing the ground for similar growth in our children.

These principles are the foundation of *Mindful Parent Happy Child*. They are easy to understand, and the intention behind them is clear:

> *to raise children with happy hearts, who feel secure within themselves and thrive*
> *to transform families, communities, schools, and society*

Mindful parenting begins when we set our intentions to cultivate awareness, self-understanding, and compassion toward ourselves and our children. *Mindful Parent Happy Child* supports this process of cultivation because we know that a deep and secure parent-child connection is the basis of a caring, just, and sustainable world.

Principle 1: All Adults Are Parents

Many people have a role in shaping a child's self-image and worldview. On a typical day, a child can encounter adults who model a variety of behaviors and attitudes—teachers, neighbors, coaches, doctors, their friends' parents, and strangers who are waiting next to them in the checkout line. These adults communicate information that children absorb and use to interpret the world and themselves. This communication plays a critical role in shaping your child's values and self-concept.

Many parents underestimate the impact others have on their children. It is also true that adults without children frequently underestimate the powerful influence they can have on children. The briefest interactions can be significant in a child's experience. This is one of the reasons I recommend that *all* adults see themselves as parents. We all are responsible for raising children, regardless of whether they are related by blood, legal adoption, school, or other.

The Community Garden

Have you ever been a member of a community garden? Members of the neighborhood cooperate in nurturing the garden, irrespective of who planted what. As a participant you may not have planted the many seeds or seedlings that inhabit the garden, but you do play an active role with others to help it all grow. To enable a bountiful harvest, everyone takes responsibility for what has been planted. At harvest time everyone benefits and celebrates.

The garden metaphor illustrates the first principle. As a child journeys along life's path, every adult rightly shares in the responsibilities of parenting. This principle encourages all adults to make a personal commitment to engage with every child in positive, nurturing ways. It reminds us that we have a responsibility to help all children plot, sow, and grow good seeds within themselves and in their world.

> *"It takes a village to raise a child"*
> –African proverb

We often take for granted that parents decide what kind of family they want to raise, but the first principle pushes each of us to become more involved in this process. *All Adults Are Parents* is a hyperbole that challenges us to share the work of child rearing—regardless of whether we have our own offspring. Whether the children we are relating to belong to us or someone else, you and I have the power to provide them with protection, support, encouragement, and guidance. Each of us has the capacity to influence how

Even the briefest interactions can be significant and influential in a child's experience.

well or how poorly the children in our communities grow, and we do ourselves and our neighbors a disservice if we let our efforts to create a better world fail to include how we attend to and interact with children.

This first principle inspires us to be more personally and socially aware in our interactions with children. It may take a village to raise a child, but it takes mindful adults within that village to raise children who will thrive and, in turn, give themselves the responsibility of growing a better world.

Principle 2: Parent-Child Connectedness Grows Happy Children

Mindfully tending the parent-child connection optimizes a child's development of healthy values and attributes, such as the following:

- stable feelings of safety, value, and worth
- personal strengths and life skills
- the ability to relate well to others
- capacities for empathy and compassion
- enthusiasm and zest for life
- self-confidence
- creativity and curiosity
- kindness and generosity
- a strong sense of personal and social responsibility

Like any good garden, a healthy parent-child connection must be tended with the right tools and growth-producing agents. Think of the parent-child connection as the soil that is purposefully prepared and maintained by you, the mindful parent. This soil, when healthy, is the dependable

It may take a village to raise a child, but it takes mindful adults within that village to raise children who will thrive and, in turn, give themselves the responsibility of growing a better world.

and loving medium in which your child is rooted; through it he or she receives vital care and nurturing. Capacities for healthy relationships with self and others can propagate in this soil, flower, and bear good fruit.

Moments of parent-child connection can give children a deep-felt sense that they are physically and emotionally safe, cared for, and valued. As mindful parents, we want to provide as many of these moments as possible over the course of our child's development.

The Parent-Child Connection Can Foster Secure Attachment

A stable and supportive parent-child connection enables children to develop what family and child counselors call *secure attachment*. "Attachment" refers to a child's instinctive bond to caregiving adults, a bond that helps to ensure a child's survival and development. A close parent-child connection supports the development of this bond and increases the likelihood that a child will mature into a healthy, happy adult. Without secure attachment from birth onward, a child is more vulnerable to distress, discouragement, and engagement in high-risk behaviors.

How do we know this? In the late 1940s, a British psychoanalyst named John Bowlby studied what effect early parent-child experiences had on children's behavior. Before Bowlby came along, it was commonly believed that as long children's basic physical needs were met, they would, in most cases, grow up to be well-adjusted, productive members of society.

In addition, as recently as the 1970s, hospitals did not allow parents to stay with their children because it was commonly believed that their presence would somehow im-

Like any good garden, a healthy parent-child connection must be tended with the right tools and growth-producing agents.

pede healing. As Bowlby studied the impact hospitalization had on young children, he discovered that such beliefs were mistaken (Bowlby,1969/1982). His research led to dramatic changes in how infants and children are cared for in our society.

"The degree of a child's attachment to her parent is shaped by the quality of sensitivity, attunement, and responsivity of the parent."
–Ruth P. Newton

Bowlby observed that when a caregiver fails to respond to signals indicating a child's need for comfort, the child initially reacts with displays of *protest*, then *despair*, and finally *detachment*. Children who have repeated experiences of detachment are more likely to have difficulty establishing stable and secure relationships in life.

Bowlby's findings led to further research by scientists like Harry Harlow, who is best known for his research with rhesus monkeys (Bowlby, 1988b). Harlow's "Contact Comfort" study described the behavior and development of an infant monkey raised in the presence of two artificial "mothers," both made of wire and shaped like adult monkeys. The hard, cold wire of one of the mothers was left exposed to the baby, but it was rigged to dispense milk. The other wire mother was wrapped with cloth, which made it softer and warmer to the touch. The baby fed from the mother that gave milk, but otherwise spent all remaining time with the cloth-covered surrogate.

Harlow's experiment demonstrated something that has been repeatedly confirmed by studies of children who lack sufficient caregiver attention: Repeated, frequent commu-

"Attachment" refers to a child's instinctive bond to caregiving adults, a bond that helps to ensure a child's survival and development.

A child's attachment to a primary caregiver plays a major role in the organization of brain development and critical mental functions related to attention and emotional regulation.

nicative interactions involving touch with a predictably warm, comforting, and secure adult are essential to a child's healthy development.

Later, Mary Ainsworth's "Strange Situation" study (1978) identified three distinct *styles of attachment* fostered in the relationship between parent and child. They are *secure, insecure-avoidant,* and *insecure-ambivalent.*

- Securely attached children are more likely to be resilient, curious, self-aware, secure in relationships, and confident of their ability to influence others. They display empathy, mutuality in relationship, and competence in social situations.

- Children with insecure-avoidant or insecure-ambivalent experiences of attachment are more susceptible to, among other things, low self-confidence, anxiety, ineffective emotional regulation, and internal conflicts that can lead to problems with personal coping and relationships.

A fourth style of attachment was later identified by a student of Ainsworth's, Mary Main (1990). Main identified an attachment style resulting from more severe abuse and/or neglect, which she described as *disorganized/disoriented.*

- A child with disorganized/disoriented attachment can be overly passive and dependent, have difficulty managing and overcoming difficult situations, display erratic emotional reactions and poor coherence of thought, and be incapable of emotional closeness.

A newborn comes into the world instinctively prepared to bond with his or her primary caregivers [1]. The attachment bond between parent and child is formed when this instinct is met with responsive care and attention. This is nature's way of keeping a child physically safe and psychologically secure while he or she learns to relate to others and otherwise adapt to the many experiences and challenges of life [2].

Children who experience a deficit of responsive care and attention are more likely to develop an *avoidant* attachment style. When primary caregivers are repeatedly unresponsive or insensitive to a child's needs and feelings, this encourages a baseline pattern of thought, emotional expression, and behavior in which the child avoids intimacy and close emotional connection [3].

Children who experience inconsistent, incongruous, and frequently reactive communication from primary caregivers can develop an *ambivalent*, anxious attachment style. Repeated experiences of inconsistent and unreliable care and unpredictable, emotionally charged reactions can foster in them a fundamental sense of insecurity and uncertainty in relation to him- or herself and others.

Children frequently subjected to chaotic, overwhelming, or terrifying experiences in their relationships with primary caregivers can develop a *disorganized*[4] attachment style. The attachment instinct drives them to be close to their caregivers for purposes of safety and security, but as they reach out for care and attention, they are met with reactions that arouse feelings of alarm and insecurity. This double bind greatly increases the risk that they will develop maladaptive ways of thinking, feeling, behaving, and engaging socially that will persist throughout their lifetime.

Children cared for by adults who are more attuned, balanced, and coherent[3] within themselves and in their connections and communications with others are more likely to be *securely attached*. They are more likely to be secure within themselves and appropriately flexible and responsive in their social relationships.

You can find a powerful illustration and discussion of the power of the attachment bond between parent and child by viewing the "Still Face Experiment" on line at www.youtube.com/watch?v=apzXGEbZht0 (Tronich, 2007; copyright by Zero To Three). I encourage you to watch it.

Securely attached children do better in life.

Understanding attachment and how to foster secure attachment with children is now a primary concern of parent education and training programs around the world.

The Happy Child

Alan Sroufe and colleagues with the *Minnesota Parent-Child Project* performed a twenty-six-year study of mother-child attachment interactions. This long-term study followed infants into adulthood and found–not surprisingly–that securely attached children showed better emotional regulation as adults than did their less secure cohorts (Sroufe, et al., 2005).

Research has repeatedly confirmed that securely attached children do better in life. Children who enjoy a secure attachment with their parents and primary caregivers are more likely to exhibit these positive traits:

- higher scores on standardized tests that measure capacities related to cognition
- more effective cooperation with teachers and other authority figures
- more interest in the mastery of games
- attraction to relationships with other children who also possess qualities of secure attachment

Securely attached children tend to do better in school, approach life with greater optimism, more easily develop a positive self-concept and identity, and are more likely to show resilience in the often choppy waters of adolescent relationships. In short, such children are generally happier and more successful—and it all springs from the fertile ground of a solid parent-child connection.

"Today, it is widely accepted that children have an absolute requirement for safe, ongoing physical and emotional closeness, and that we ignore this only at great cost."
–Susan Johnson

Understanding attachment and how to foster secure attachment with children is now a primary concern of parent education and training programs around the world. *Mindful Parent Happy Child* shares this interest and provides a framework to actively approach the task of developing more secure attachments between parents and their children through practices of mindfulness. A mindful parent-child connection provides the soil in which roots of secure attachment are more likely to flourish.
It works like this:

Did You Know

Did You Know? A child's attachments are formed by seven months of age.

- Through mindfulness practice you can cultivate a more stable and secure relationship with yourself.
- Connecting with yourself in this way allows for enhanced self-regulation–of your own body's needs, sensations, thoughts, emotions, and automatic responses–when you are interacting with your child.
- As the quality of your availability to your child is enhanced, so is your ability to "attune" to your child's emotional cues and signals.
- Cultivated mindfulness becomes the groundwork for a healthier parent-child connection that positively influences the quality of the attachment bond you have with your child.
- This attachment bond influences how well a child

attunes and responds to her- or himself and others and effectively meets the circumstances of life.

Principle 3: Mindful Parenting Is a Life Practice

Like a devoted gardener who consistently pays attention to what is needed to foster healthier growth throughout the seasons, mindful parents consistently pay attention to being an attuned and nurturing presence throughout their children's development.

This principle speaks to the transformational character of consistent, long-term applications of mindful parenting practices. Like a devoted gardener who consistently pays attention to what is needed to foster healthier growth throughout the seasons, mindful parents consistently pay attention to being an attuned and nurturing presence throughout their children's development.

While some parenting books and educational programs are better than others, all of them exist to give helpful information about the practical realities of child rearing. Some can help parents learn how to keep their children well and well-adjusted by teaching such things as how to care for a newborn, how to regulate a child's sleep patterns, and how to identify which children's products are safe. Others teach techniques for containing or controlling the behavior of children. They describe how to administer timeouts; use behavioral contracts, "feeling" charts, and token economy systems; and interact with your children in order to get them to behave in more respectful or responsible ways. Most parenting education today focuses on *information* related to good child care and/or *transactions* that help to more effectively contain and control your child's behavior.

While it is helpful to be knowledgeable about the care and management of children through such programs, it is far from sufficient. With *Mindful Parent Happy Child* our primary concern is not in teaching information or guiding transactions; instead, it is the personal *transformation* of the parent and the parent-child relationship that comes from mindfulness practice. Transformation is about deeper change. It moves us first to look beyond the information we can obtain about parenting and toward the cultivation of security, calmness, empathy, and greater capacities for intimacy within ourselves.

This is the primary meaning behind principle 3: Parental self-work is a prerequisite for happier, healthier children. Ultimately you will be a better parent if you *first* do the work necessary to better tend to your own inner garden.

Mindful Parent Happy Child is about teaching parents how to watch their automatic thoughts, emotions, and behavioral patterns through mindfulness practice. Over time such practices stimulate change in the brain's neural pathways and other structures. Using mindfulness practice to help you "rewire" your brain in ways that will yield a better parent-child connection takes consistent effort, and such effort will often be met with challenges along the way. Learning how to be present and not reactive when chaos ensues is developed with time, a lifetime.

Be "PRESENT"

The inner skills and tools related to cultivating mindfulness require daily attention. The word "PRESENT" provides a handy acronym to help you remember the elements of this principle and ensure daily mindful parenting practice. Being PRESENT as a parent includes practicing the following:

- *Patience:*
  Patience is the staying power necessary to encourage parents over time not to give up on themselves or their chil-

Transformation is about deeper change. It moves us to look beyond the information we can obtain about parenting and toward the cultivation of security, calmness, empathy, and greater capacities for intimacy within ourselves.

dren. Without patience, impatience breeds and manifests as judgment, rigidity, anxiety, discouragement, and failure. Patience fosters flexibility, letting go, openness, trust, and confidence. Patience is a gift mindful parents must give themselves in order to stay in the process of their personal growth. Mindful parenting develops with time from consistent and persistent practice, through trials and errors, and periods of slow progress.

- *Receptivity:*

Receptivity means being open to seeing the truth about yourself and the areas in which you need to grow and change as a parent. Receptivity helps you become aware of and attuned to your own thoughts, feelings, and reactions, as well as to those of your child. Being receptive means being available to learn new ways of doing things that will benefit your relationships with the children in your life.

- *Equanimity:*

Equanimity is an approach to life that serves as an equalizer of all things. Issues and situations that arise are neither good nor bad; they are part of the ebb and flow of life. Equanimity is seeing a flower and a weed as having equal value, one not better than the other. Equanimity refers to your ability to maintain inner calm even when a storm of chaos surrounds you. In times of joy, equanimity serves to keep you from becoming attached or dependent upon the good feelings because *these too shall pass.* As a parent, staying emotionally balanced allows you to *respond* to your child, rather than *react.* Equanimity will help you remain grounded and keep extreme emotions at bay.

Patience fosters flexibility, letting go, openness, trust, and confidence.

- *Sensing:*

   In the context of mindful parenting, *sensing* means remaining aware of the physical senses of touch, taste, smell, hearing, and sight, as well as other senses such as intuition and empathy. Practicing awareness in all of the areas that participate in the experience of being yourself will enable you to more consciously regulate physiological and emotional responses so that you can behave in ways that are more flexible and adaptive to the needs of your child.

- *Effort:*

   Thomas Edison once said, *"Opportunity is missed by most people because it is dressed in overalls and looks like work."* Practicing anything requires effort, especially when we are working to make changes in habitual patterns of reactivity and negativity. *Effort* is energy in motion. Putting *Mindful Parent Happy Child* teachings into practice involves things such as remembering to slow down and breathe before reacting, and thinking strategically and deliberately, instead of running on automatic. It takes effort to become and remain aware and attuned with yourself and your children.

- *Nonjudgment:*

   Practicing *nonjudgment* means being gentle with yourself when you find yourself not being the parent you hoped to be. Practicing nonjudgment requires relentless tracking of judgmental thoughts that swarm in our minds. Judgment is evident in how harshly we criticize, diminish, or discount ourselves and others. It produces shame and is the opposite of compassion; it serves no one well. A cornerstone of personal change involves learning, through mindfulness practice, to neutralize and eventually let go of the critical judge

Practicing nonjudgment means being gentle with yourself when you find yourself not being the parent you hoped to be.

that resides within us. Perhaps, most important, practicing nonjudgement includes not judging yourself when you catch yourself being judging!

- *Time:*

   Practicing mindful parenting requires a conscious use of *time*. This does not mean that you necessarily have to find time for more formal approaches to mindfulness, such as meditation or journal keeping. Rather, it means that you intentionally *take the time* to consciously "check in" with yourself, to be aware of when and how you direct your attention. You can find time for such practice while in the shower, walking the dog, sitting in traffic, doing the dishes, or making the bed. This kind of time can and should be taken often while you are engaged in the regular activities of daily living.

   When we live outside our own values, we feel off kilter. When we commit ourselves to something we believe in, it becomes a value. Incorporating the Three Principles of Mindful Parenting into your life will provide you a solid foundation as a mindful parent, and further enhance your moral compass.

   You do not have to accept these principles in order to be a mindful parent, but before you decide to accept or reject them, try them on and see how they fit. Mindful parenting is a practice that gently develops into something we become, not something we do. As you remind yourself to remain PRESENT throughout your day, in time you will see the payoff; you will watch your children become the joyful and resilient people they are capable of being.

You do not have to accept these principles in order to be a mindful parent, but before you decide to accept or reject them, try them on and see how they fit.

Tending Your Garden

I enjoy gardening. It is an important part of my lineage. Both of my grandmothers were wonderful gardeners, growing raspberries for Thanksgiving pie, and summertime squash. My father plants a garden every spring that is the envy of friends and neighbors. My sister plants flowers, sweet peas, and a wide assortment of vegetables. My brother tends to his small plot of grapevines for homemade wine. In my garden I planted all my favorite fruit trees: avocado, apple, nectarine, plum, orange, and apricot. I also grow the herbs I most enjoy cooking with.

Gardening terms like *seed, cultivate, sow, harvest, till, root, plot, fertilize,* and *bloom* easily translate to child rearing. Plants are living things. Like our children, who have different temperaments and personalities, each plant variety requires specific care. Gardeners pay close attention to their plants—whether they are African violets, roses, or cacti. They read their signs and gauge their needs. Plants tell you what they need, and so do children.

Like plants in a garden, children are born with an instinct to survive. They come through the womb with built-in communication systems that we must learn to understand in order to help them survive and grow up well and well-adjusted. A mindful parent learns to read the signals his or her child uses to communicate.

From infancy through adolescence and beyond, children normally do their best to get your attention and let you know what they need. At each stage of maturity a new set of needs emerges. Just as there will come a time when a seedling may require a bigger pot, there also will come a time when a toddler will need to learn how to establish

Like plants in a garden, children are born with an instinct to survive.

and negotiate healthy boundaries with others. The fact is, if we neglect the seeds we sow, their potential for growing and blooming into full maturity can be compromised. They can become stunted and sickly, unable to flower or produce well. With severe neglect, they can fail to thrive and then die.

The three principles of Mindful Parenting remind us that each new day brings with it the responsibility to tend to the needs of children—not just those in our own garden, but those in every kind of garden. *Mindful Parent Happy Child* invites you to work at living these principles each day—in your home, at your jobs, and with strangers. In the long run, you will be making an enormous contribution to ensuring a more peaceful world for all children, and their children, as well.

The fact is, if we neglect the seeds we sow, their potential for growing and blooming into full maturity can be compromised.

Quick Glance: Chapter Three

The Three Principles:
- All adults are parents.
- Parent-child connectedness grows happy children.
- Mindful Parenting is a life practice.

⇒ Parents are like gardeners, tending the children in their care. As human beings, we possess a variety of seeds we can sow within ourselves and in others, whether they be seeds of love, hate, joy, fear, generosity, or greed. If we want to raise a loving child, we need to plant and tend the seeds that grow love.

⇒ As adults, we are faced with the task of taking over and becoming the responsible caretakers of our own gardens. This requires that we regularly take a step back and observe for ourselves what is thriving and blossoming, and what is withering or dying on the vine.

All Adults are Parents

⇒ Many parents underestimate the impact others have on their children. It is also true that adults without children frequently underestimate the powerful influence they can have on children. The briefest interactions can be significant in a child's experience.

⇒ This first principle inspires us to be more personally and socially aware in our interactions with children. It may take a village to raise a child, but it takes mindful adults within that village to raise children who will thrive and, in turn, give themselves the responsibility of growing a better world.

Parent-Child Connectedness Grows Happy Children

⇒ "Attachment" refers to a child's instinctive bond with caregiving adults, a bond that helps to ensure a child's survival and development. A close parent-child connection supports the development of this bond and increases the likelihood that a child will mature into a healthy, happy adult.

⇒ Bowlby and Robertson observed that when a caregiver fails to respond to signals indicating a child's need for comfort, the child initially reacts with displays of *protest*, then *despair*, and finally *detachment*.

⇒ It is not always the *amount* of time spent with your child, but the *kind* of time that grows the parent-child connection. Intentional moments of attunement, closeness, and responsiveness give children a deep-felt sense that they are physically and emotionally safe, cared for, and valued.

⇒ Securely attached children tend to do better in school, approach life with greater optimism, more easily develop a positive self-concept and identity, and are more likely to show resilience in the often choppy waters of adolescent relationships. In short, such children are generally happier and more successful—and it all springs from the fertile ground of a solid parent-child connection.

Mindful Parenting Is a Life Practice

⇒ This is the primary meaning behind principle 3: Parental self-work is a prerequisite for happier, healthier children. Ultimately you will be a better parent if you *first* do the work necessary to better tend to your own inner garden.

⇒ *Mindful Parent Happy Child* is about teaching parents how to watch their automatic thoughts, emotions, and behavioral patterns through mindfulness practice. Over time such practices stimulate change in the brain's neural pathways and other structures.

⇒ The inner skills and tools related to cultivating mindfulness require daily attention. The word "PRESENT" provides a handy acronym to help you remember the elements of this principle to ensure a daily mindful parenting practice. They are Patience, Receptivity, Equanimity, Sensing, Effort, Nonjudgment, and Time.

"Allow emotions to move within

and through you like waves that

roll onto the shore and wash

back out into the ocean."

Chapter Four
Becoming a Mindful Parent:
The Three-Phase Model of Practice

Mindful Awareness
Self-Intervention
Deliberate Action

I n most parent education programs the focus is on *how to change the child*. The learning objectives are about teaching parents methods of communication and intervention that will result in the modification of a child's undesirable patterns of thinking, feeling, and behaving. When it comes to helping parents cultivate a more stable, secure, and adaptive way of being—which is the first and most basic place to begin when interacting with your child—there is often little or no guidance.

The model presented in this chapter encourages a more radical (i.e. beginning with the "roots") approach to parenting. The model is designed to help you apply principles of mindfulness in the context of your everyday interactions with your child in order to strengthen the *parent-child connection*.

The model is easy to learn. As you practice it, step by step, you will interrupt and redirect your brain's habitual and reactive ways of responding to yourself and others and cultivate deeper and more comprehensive levels of self-attunement. As your practice continues, you can anticipate feeling more centered, confident, and effective in your parenting, and you will notice changes in how you and your child interact with each other. Most important, you will be doing exactly what is required to begin creating a more excellent environment for the healthy and happy development of your children.

Introducing the Model

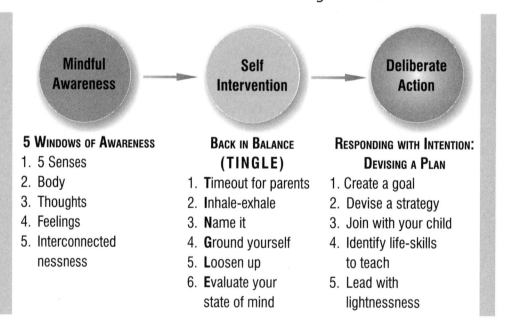

5 WINDOWS OF AWARENESS
1. 5 Senses
2. Body
3. Thoughts
4. Feelings
5. Interconnected nessness

BACK IN BALANCE (TINGLE)
1. **T**imeout for parents
2. **I**nhale-exhale
3. **N**ame it
4. **G**round yourself
5. **L**oosen up
6. **E**valuate your state of mind

RESPONDING WITH INTENTION: DEVISING A PLAN
1. Create a goal
2. Devise a strategy
3. Join with your child
4. Identify life-skills to teach
5. Lead with lightnessness

The purpose of the *Mindful Parent Happy Child* model is to help you, the parent, maintain and strengthen the quality of the parent-child connection. As noted previously, such a connection with your child begins with you developing a more highly attuned connection with yourself. As you increase self-attunement, you invite a deeper and stronger connection with your child. In other words, as you become more *self-connected*, you can become more adequately *parent-child connected*.

The model guides you to follow a progressive sequence that will carry you through three different phases of mindfulness:

- In the first phase, *Mindful Awareness*, you will apply techniques that help you develop awareness of your whole self (senses, body, mind, emotions, and interconnectedness) using what I call the *Five Windows of Awareness*.

- In the second phase, *Self-Intervention*, you will use your awareness to disrupt reactions that might threaten or damage the security and integrity of the connection you have with yourself and your child. In this phase, you can use six easy-to-remember steps to help you settle down and regain a balanced state so that you can think more rationally and effectively.

- In the third and final phase, *Deliberate Action*, you will create an attuned and solution-oriented plan designed to help your children continue to live in an environment where they can feel *safe, secure, respected, heard, and loved. If there was damage done to the parent-child connection, this is the time to make a repair.*

As you increase self-attunement you invite a deeper and stronger connection with your child.

By using this model in situations that are grounded in mindful awareness, self-intervention, and deliberate action—be it setting limits, negotiating a consequence for poor behavior, or disrupting a sibling squabble—you will be better prepared to:

- create an environment for learning and self-reflection
- model self-regulating behaviors, emotions, and stability
- reinforce emotional security
- demonstrate positive communication
- teach problem-solving skills

The *Mindful Parent Happy Child* Model can be depicted in this way:

5 Windows of Awareness

Mindful Awareness

- 5 Senses
- Body
- Thoughts
- Feelings
- Interconnectedness

Phase 1: Mindful Awareness

In our fast-paced world, we seem to be plugged in to just about everything—Wi-Fi, iPods, iPads, cell phones, BlackBerries, Facebook, Twitter, Instant Messaging, and more. As mindful parents, it is important to keep this explosion of personal technology in proper perspective. Wonderfully, technology enables us to have immediate access to information and to communicate with greater frequency and immediacy with family, friends, colleagues, and strangers around the world. But over-depending on such technology to mediate our connections with each other puts the irreplaceable parent-child connection at risk.

The purpose of this first phase, *Mindful Awareness*, is to give you self-awareness skills that will help you stay connected—or plugged in—to *you* in the present moment. Developing a practice of Mindful Awareness will help you:

- prevent feelings of depression or being overwhelmed that can be caused by negative ruminations about the past, or greatly reduce anxious anticipations about what might happen in the future
- develop a deeper and more comprehensive awareness of your "self"
- better understand and integrate your inner world so that you can relate more fully and effectively with your children

The Five Windows of Awareness

Developing your mindful parenting practice involves attending to five different areas of your "whole" self, which I refer to as the Five Windows:

1. your five senses *(taste, touch, sound, sight, and smell)*
2. your body *(your physical self and its sensations)*
3. your thoughts *(perceptions, beliefs, assumptions, and judgments)*
4. your emotions *(including hurt, anger, shame, fear, loneliness, guilt, comfort, peace, happiness, and joy)*

5. your interconnections with others *(especially your experiences of developing and sharing an attuned state with another person)*

Using the *Five Windows of Awareness* keeps us on a path of connection with ourselves and others, and that connection is the starting point from which positive change becomes possible.

Window 1: Your Senses

The senses are the means by which we see, hear, smell, taste, and touch. Each sense collects information about the world and detects changes within the body. Our sense organs (nose, eyes, ears, tongue, and skin) are constantly taking in information and sending it to the brain for processing. When any one of these sense organs becomes stimulated, the receptors send nerve impulses along sensory nerves to the brain. Your brain processes this information and tells you what the stimulus is. For example, when you hear your child cry, your sound receptors are stimulated by countless sound waves. When these signals reach the cerebral cortex, you become aware of the sound and identify it as your baby crying.

Learning by direct experience—for example, trying to walk on hot coals—is definitely one way to heighten your awareness to the fact that you have sensory receptors. However, this is certainly not what it should take to awaken you to the present moment. The practice of mindful awareness is a much less painful approach!

At this point I invite you to open yourself to this kind of direct experience. Stop reading and interpreting the written word for a little while, and turn your attention to your five senses. The following exercise will help you focus upon each of your senses so that you can begin developing greater awareness of each of them and the information they make available to you.

EXERCISE

Give the following sensory experiments a try. As you read the instructions about each particular sense, focus your attention on the sense and the experience(s) it is giving you in the moment.

First, turn your attention to . . .

Taste: Keeping your attention on your tongue, focus on what you taste. As you focus your attention, taste becomes magnified, and you may have to resist a sudden urge to brush your teeth! Be still, and keep your attention on what you taste. Try to name it. Is it bitter? salty? sweet? Try to detect the subtlest flavors.

Now turn your attention to . . .

Touch: Focus your attention on your fingertips. If you are holding this book, keep your attention focused on the sensation at your fingertips, or touch something close by and hold your attention there, at the point of touch. If your mind wanders, simply bring it back to the sensation at your fingertips.

Name the sensation. Is it rough? smooth? What is the temperature? Is it warm? cool? Try to describe this sensation in a sentence.

Next, turn your attention to . . .

Sight: Bring your attention to what you see. Consider an object as if you are seeing it for the first time. Use your sight to examine the object carefully, and notice its details. The object can be something as ordinary as your carpet or your knee. Name what you see. Say the color out loud. Name what you notice is different.

Now, turn your attention to . . .

Sound: With your attention focused on what you hear, name the sound. Try to focus first on what you hear closest to you. Really hear the sounds and notice them. Next, do the same thing with sounds that are farther away. What are you hearing that you did not notice earlier? Name it and stay with it for a minute or so as you remain alert and ready to hear new sounds.

Finally, turn your attention to . . .

Smell: Without changing your breathing, focus your attention on the smells around you. If there is a combination of odors and aromas, try to differentiate one from another. Name what you smell. Is it strong? subtle? fruity? spicy? earthy? familiar? unfamiliar? Ask yourself if it smells pleasant or unpleasant to you.

Your five senses are just *one* window of Mindful Awareness that you can look into at any time. Practice these simple sensory awareness exercises throughout the day over a few weeks' time. Soon you will find that you are more conscious of these five important senses and what they can tell you.

Window 2: Your Body

Many of us tend to take our bodies for granted until we catch a cold, cut our thumb, or tweak our back. We can be catapulted into awareness of our body by the pain or inconvenience that accompanies such minor nuisances. But what about less obvious health issues—potentially deadly ones—wherein symptoms of pain or dysfunction are not as apparent?

Our body is more than a vehicle that gets us from here to there. Remaining unaware of your body is like driving your car without paying attention to an illuminated warning light on the dashboard. The light might be signaling the need for an oil change, but it also might indicate that your engine is about to seize up. If you aren't paying attention to your car, you may not be able to interpret the engine light appropriately, or worse, not even notice it. Such mindlessness while driving can put you and your passengers at risk! The same goes with your body; if you don't pay attention to its signals, you will not be at your best for your children.

The dragon lady
Our body sends myriad signals through the central nervous system to our brain. If I do not pay attention to what my brain is telling me, I am prone to being overtaken by hun-

No pill or
supplement can
replace good
sleep, exercise,
balanced meals,
and a few good
minutes of
meditation.

ger. My husband refers to me as his "wilting flower" when I fail to be mindful of my hunger signals. At such times the warning light is flashing on the dashboard, but I don't see it! My husband is being too kind. Believe me when I tell you that when my blood sugar gets too low, I am no "wilting flower." Rather I am more like a huge dragon with a sharp, three-pronged tongue that spews fire and hot coals!

Paying attention to your body and its signals will allow you to stay physiologically balanced and at your best. It is easier to regulate your thoughts and emotions when you are well-nourished and rested. This being said, if you are anything like many of the well-meaning parents I have known and worked with, to get through your busy day you will frequently ignore your body's signals and compromise your physical and emotional needs.

In the midst of life's busyness it is easy to cut corners. Busyness can cause us to neglect our health and well-being in countless ways. We can find ourselves drinking too much coffee in an attempt to counter a persistent sleep deficit. We can fall into a bad habit of gulping down a nutritionally deficient fast food meal instead of preparing home cooked, balanced fare. We can end up treating our bodies like machines, giving them just enough to keep them moving. We may even promise ourselves that tomorrow we will take better care of ourselves by getting to bed earlier, eating more healthful food, or exercising; but tomorrow will certainly bring another unexpected appointment or crisis. Such behaviors represent mindless self neglect that, over time, negatively impact the parent-child connection.

Practicing awareness of our physical selves requires more from us than taking a daily vitamin as we run out the door in the morning. Attention to our body gives us opportunities to observe and change such mindless behaviors. No pill or supplement can replace good sleep, exercise, balanced meals, and a few good minutes of meditation. Mindfulness and living mindfully presents us with opportunities to better identify how our body feels and what it needs—in this present moment. Maintaining a poor connection with our physical selves will negatively impact our relationships with children. Paying attention to our physical needs and the choices we make for our bodies while we live on-the-go with our children is essential to good parenting.

A single dad doing his best
Ben, who had been widowed for two years, was doing his best to juggle everything. He was the sole parent and primary adult in the lives of his nine-year-old twins, Gina and Jill. Ben worked for himself, so he could be somewhat flexible with his hours and participate in their many school-related and recreational activities. Ben's devotion to his children was obvious, but he was chronically tired and concerned about how this was affecting his parenting. To get through each day, Ben acknowledged he was cutting some crucial health corners. He told me, *"If my wife saw what I was feeding our girls, she would be furious."* Ben served takeout most nights and permitted the girls to eat cookies with breakfast in an attempt to keep them happy. He allowed them to spend long hours in front of the television, rather than taking them to the park or beach, because this seemed to keep them satisfied. He had begun to question his ability to take care of them and was riddled with guilt and worry.

While I was talking with Ben, I discovered that in his efforts to be there for Gina and Jill, he was not taking care of himself, especially his physical needs. His body was slowly

Paying attention to our physical needs and the choices we make for our bodies while we live on the go with our children is essential to good parenting.

giving out. I asked him to identify daily habits and routines that might contribute to his exhaustion and interfere with being the parent he wanted to be.

Ben's days were demanding. Three nights a week Ben worked into the evening, leaving the girls with a sitter until he got home at around 8:30 P.M. On the days Ben didn't work late, he shuttled Gina and Jill to their after-school activities and monitored their homework. When the girls were nestled in their beds, Ben understandably took what he called "me time" by winding down with a few glasses of wine and two to three hours of television. Around midnight Ben headed for bed.

As it turns out, Gina and Jill were early birds. If they had missed saying "goodnight" to their dad the night before, they would often try to make up for it by crawling into his bed around 6 A.M. Still groggy and poorly rested, he would try to hold them and talk with them. One daughter was usually hungry for breakfast while the other was ready to play. "Get up, Daddy! Get up!" they would chime, and he would drag himself out of bed to try to meet their needs for food and parental attention.

Change was on the way
By cultivating a more consistent awareness of his body—how it felt and what it was communicating—Ben taught himself to recognize when his worn-out body was beginning to cause problems for himself and his children. As he became more aware, he decided to make a few changes in how he was doing things. As a result, he began feeling more energetic and, therefore, more engaged with his girls. Here are some of the changes Ben made:

1.   He started by looking more closely at how he sched-

Did You Know

The best way to measure how much water your body needs a day is to drink 50 percent of your weight in ounces. For example if you weigh 130 pounds, then you need to drink 65 ounces of water or other fluids a day; coffee and Diet Coke don't count!

uled his day, the needs of his children, and the impact of his eating and sleeping habits.

2. He came to realize that he needed to work fewer hours in the evening. This meant he had less money to spend, but the budget deficit was somewhat offset by his less frequent use of a sitter.

3. He gave himself more relaxed time with his girls in the evening. He began to cook more dinners and enjoy family meals.

4. He rescheduled his work hours so that he could run errands while Gina and Jill were still at school.

5. He began eating better, buying fresh food and healthful snacks.

6. He bought himself a used bicycle and took his girls on bike rides for exercise.

7. Under his previous system of "me time," Ben realized that he was losing as much as two to three hours of potential sleep. Although it was a challenge at first, he began to limit his evening habit of alcohol and TV by cutting everything in half: half the alcohol and half the television time. After a few weeks, Ben discovered that he liked the feeling of renewed energy this gave him, so he decided to change his schedule even more. When he put the girls to bed, he did things to wind down that did not include alcohol or television; he worked on his schedule, showered, read a book or magazine, or called a friend. He found that his new behaviors took better care of his body, and he felt more vitalized as a result.

8. Ben also began to check in with himself throughout the day, doing mini body-awareness scans. This

helped him stay aware of his physical needs and prevented him from falling back into old patterns.

Ben learned that mindful parenting involves learning to pay conscious attention to your body, including specific areas that experience tension and pain. To parent mindfully and maintain the parent-child connection, it is important to remain aware of your own body's rhythms and signals. This will keep you better hydrated, nourished, and rested.

Many parents race through the day driven by a mental list in the back of their minds: bills that need to be paid, recycling to be disposed of, an overflowing litter box to clean, and *"Oh!' Someone's birthday is coming up, but whose and when?"* All the while, lunches need to be packed, homework checked, baths taken, and good-night kisses planted on sweet cheeks. In the bustle of such activities, is your lack of body awareness compromising the connection between you and your child? Throughout the day stop and check in with yourself: Are you drinking enough water? Getting enough rest? Are you giving yourself small breaks throughout the day to sit still and let your body relax? Are you hungry? Are you getting enough exercise?

Helloooooo body!
Attending classes in yoga, Tai Chi, or Qi Gong are excellent ways to work physical awareness into your week, reduce stress, and ward off depression, but not everyone has time for such activities. When you are busy but you still want to check in with your body, take a few moments to sit or lie down in a comfortable place, close your eyes, turn on soothing music, and do five minutes of relaxed breathing. Do what you can during your day to make mindfulness of your

body a routine. It's important that you develop your own *practice* of body mindfulness, one that works for you and your lifestyle, so that you will remain balanced throughout your day.

One method for fitting body awareness into your day is to use questions to help you check in with yourself, increase your physical self-awareness, and to perform a body scan to assess whether something more is needed for you to stay in balance physically.

Such questions are a way of saying, *"Hello Body! How are you doing right now?"*

1. Am I thirsty? How much have I had to drink today?
2. Am I hungry? What have I eaten so far today?
3. Am I tired? How much sleep have I gotten this week?
4. Am I achy, tight, or tingly anywhere? If so, describe it.
5. Am I having regular bathroom breaks and bowel movements?
6. Am I clenching my teeth, tightening my shoulders, biting my nails, or exhibiting other signs of chronic nervousness?
7. Where am I feeling stress in my body?

Think of times and places where you can use these questions to do a quick check-in with your body. Perhaps you can use them while you are:

- driving in your car
- taking a shower
- standing in line
- sitting in traffic
- setting the table

- vacuuming the floor
- packing lunches
- awakening
- watering plants
- watching commercials

Write down ten other times in the course of your day that you might say "hello" to your body:

1.
2.
3.
4.
5.
6.
7.
8.
9.
10.

These are simple ways to begin developing awareness of your physical self. With daily practice you will be better attuned to your body's needs before you turn into a sharp-tongued, fire-breathing dragon.

Window 3: Your Thinking

There are many kinds of thoughts and types of thinking. Human beings ponder, process, analyze, hope, believe, ruminate, muse, assume, contemplate, imagine, reflect, evaluate, and more. Our thoughts can be positive, negative, or neutral; they can support and stimulate a wide variety of emotional states. They can also cause us to feel helpless and hopeless, victimized and fearful. Being aware of our thoughts allows us to begin evaluating them. What we think affects everything: our emotions, behaviors, physical and spiritual health. Evaluating our thoughts opens us to the possibility that our thoughts may not be grounded in reality. It can be a useless and destructive habit to believe everything we think! Why? In large part, so much of what we think is linked to either an unconscious belief from our past or an inaccurate assumption we are making in the present.

Until we are aware of our thoughts, they are like an unmonitored child in a candy store. Anything is up for the grabbing! When we learn to become mindful of our thoughts in the present moment, we expose ourselves to an internal dialogue that is doing one of two things, directing us well or directing us poorly. It can be rather shocking to observe all the thinking, analyzing, assuming, judging, ruminating, and what I call "negative futurizing" we do. Awareness of our thoughts enables us to begin working with them by asking ourselves questions and reality checks: "Is this thought (or belief) a fact or fiction? How do I know?" "Is this thought supported by data, or is it fantasy?"

My personal experience
I learned a long time ago not to assume I was always accurate in *what I thought* another person was thinking, no matter how he or she behaved. Here's a great example, one you might even relate to.

In my early days of speaking, 99 percent of the people in the audience looked interested, sat up straight in their seats, raised their hands, and took copious notes. However, the one person dozing off hooked my attention. In a nanosecond I surmised that I must be a boring, lousy pre-

Until we are
aware of our
thoughts, they
are like an
unmonitored
child in a
candy store.

senter. This thought had horrifying consequences because I became mentally paralyzed by feelings of panic and self-doubt. I began stumbling over my words and corroding the wonderful flow of thought and speech I had created.

What was happening to me? Nothing, other than an old fear—hidden from my conscious mind—that remained buried deep within my implicit memory. Once fear was triggered in my primal brain, the "fight, flight, freeze" response took over, and I froze! Obviously, if I had been able to remain somewhat grounded in the reasoning center of my brain, I could have assessed the situation.

After all, the data read that 99 percent of the audience was engaged. I must not be a lousy and boring presenter. If I had not been triggered, I may have guessed at a few other reasons why an individual was dozing off during my presentation. For example, perhaps she was on antihistamines because of pollen; maybe she partied too much the night before; maybe she was a new mom and was up four times during the night; or perhaps she had just completed midterm exams. Any number of circumstances could have been factored in … if my brain had been in a balanced state. What I have now that I didn't have then was the skill of being mindful of my thoughts. This allows me to recognize a negative assumption before it carries me away into panic mode.

Minding your thoughts
As a mindful parent you know why it is so important to be aware of your thoughts. Mindfulness practice teaches us how to watch our thoughts as things that happen, and teaches us that *while we have thoughts, we do not have to believe or be passive in what we think.*

In the *Mindful Parent Happy Child* classes, parents learn how to be aware of the amazing, seemingly unstoppable gyrations of thought that some mindfulness teachers have referred to as "monkey mind." In mindfulness practice, one starts by learning to watch the activity of the mind, which at first is ordinarily scattered and unfocused. When parents find their mind uncooperative, they rush to the conclusion that they are unable to meditate. The reality is, when you are allowing yourself to be conscious of that busy brain activity of yours, you *are* meditating.

"You should rather be grateful for the weeds you have in your mind, because eventually they will enrich your practice."
–S. Suzuki

As you participate in mindfulness practice, you can learn many things:

- You can become more aware of your thoughts and more able to identify which thoughts support you in feeling good, and you can distinguish them from the thoughts that cause suffering related to negative judgments, distress, worry, frustration, and fear.
- You can identify if the thoughts you are having in the present moment are, indeed, about the present or if they are anchored more in the past or in the future.
- You can learn how to *compartmentalize* your thoughts, separating those that are related to the present situation from those that have to do with

something else, or those that are positive and con-structive from those that are not.

To increase your understanding of the link between how we think and the automatic reactions related to thoughts, imagine yourself as the parent in the following scenario:

You are about to "lose your cool" because your child is suddenly throwing a major tantrum during a grocery store's rush hour. You've seen your child do this before, and you know this can trigger a host of negative feelings and negative reactions in you and others. You are afraid that some critical, disapproving grandmother is about to turn her cart right into your aisle and give you the evil eye for not being a good mother. It doesn't help in the least that Ben and Jerry are also in your shopping basket "melting down" with your child. You hate looking like a bad parent with a problem child. You want this to stop, and the pressure is on.

Can you identify what this parent might be thinking that is causing her to feel out of control? Write down some possibilities:

1.

2.

3.

Now ask yourself: Can you identify with this parent's experience? Might you have been thinking the same thing if you had been in this parent's situation, or would your thoughts likely to have been different? Note what might have been the same or different:

1.

2.

3.

Being someone who attends to his or her thoughts—rather than someone who lives without being aware of them—is the first and most critical step in creating a deeper, more affirming connection with your children. You may have noticed that this particular Window is the largest of the other four Windows of Awareness. Training your mind to be aware of your thoughts plays a key role in the redesign and remodeling of your brain's architecture.

Finally, if you remember nothing else, remember this: in the end your style of thinking impacts you, your connection with your children, and your children's development. Your thinking is a significant factor in determining your children's predominant thoughts and feelings about themselves.

Being someone who attends to his or her thoughts—rather than someone who lives without being aware of them—is the first and most critical step in creating a deeper, more affirming connection with your children.

Delving Deeper: The Nature of Mind

Prior to 1992 the scientific community had no unifying definition of mind. Some simply equated the mind with brain activity. Others defined it as a social process that spans generations. That year, Dr. Dan Siegel (2010) organized a conversation among scientists about the relationship between the physical organ, the human brain, and the subjective nature of "mind." As a result, he came to understand the mind as the process that "regulates the flow of energy and information" within our bodies and between us and others. He developed the concept of "mindsight" as the human capacity to "sense and shape energy and information flow," which is arguably the primary purpose and function of mindfulness practice. Siegel concludes:

> "The mind is broader than the brain, revels in relationships, and is pregnant with possibilities . . . with mindsight we gain perception and knowledge of the regulation (mind), sharing (relationships), and mediating neural mechanisms (brain) at the heart of our lives. 'Our lives' means yours and mine. Mindsight takes away the superficial boundaries that separate us and enables us to see that we are each part of an interconnected flow, a wider whole."

By viewing mind, brain, and relationships as fundamentally three dimensions of one reality—of aspects of energy and information flow—we see our human experience with truly new eyes. (Siegel, 2010)

As you read this, are you aware of your thoughts right now, in this very moment? Are you completely focused on what you are reading, or is part of your mind wandering off in an entirely different direction, such as to the list of To Do's still waiting on your list? Try watching your mind's activities like you would a TV show. The program can have parts that are good, positive, and inspiring. Other parts can be harshly critical, depressing, and hopeless. Conventional wisdom tells us to watch what we say. We would certainly do better if we could learn to watch what we think.

Minding the mind with mindfulness
In my clinical practice I frequently counsel bright, creative, responsible people who inappropriately self-medicate with

prescription or street drugs, alcohol, food, porn, or computer games. Most of the time they are using these substances and activities as ways to help them cope with stress, anxiety, low self-esteem, or relational conflicts. Self-medicating never gets to the root of the problem and frequently leads to greater problems down the road. Parents who self-medicate are not only teaching unhealthy coping skills to their children, they also are unable to be present to the needs of their children, thereby damaging the process of healthy attachment.

The World Health Organization predicts that by 2020 depression will be the second greatest cause of disability and suffering in the human population. What does this say about the pressure adults feel today and their ability to handle the pressure in healthy and productive ways?

As we have seen in the foregoing discussion about attachment, environmental influences play an important role in shaping the structures of the brain. A child's relationships and circumstances significantly influence how he or she learns to think, feel, and approach life. As parents, what our thinking style is, whether our thoughts are of the "Good Ship Lollipop" or the "Black Fog of Loneliness and Despair," our style of thinking correlates strongly with how and why we feel the way we feel and behave the way we behave. Children who grow up with depressed parents are three times more likely to develop depression. The implications are clear: Depression is "contagious" (Yapko, 2009), and the transmission of depression and its crippling effects could be significantly reduced if parents and caregivers learned skills to *mind their minds with mindfulness*.

Did You Know

Repeated, excessive releases of the stress hormone cortisol can actually deaden areas of the brain, contribute to obesity, and make one more vulnerable to depression.

Children who grow up with depressed parents are three times more likely to develop depression.

People who concentrate on positive emotions have deeper relationships, higher incomes, better physical health, longer lives, and a broader and more resourceful outlook on life.

This next exercise demonstrates how certain thoughts can influence and magnify your experience. Try it and see what you notice.

EXERCISE

Wherever you are, put this book down and repeat each italicized word out loud five or six times. Repeat the words slowly, and allow them to sink in. As you do this, pay attention to the emotions and physical sensations that arise in you as you say them. Your reaction may be quite subtle or difficult to identify at first, but stay with it. When you finish repeating a word, write down the feelings that accompanied the word.

Begin by saying to yourself:
"I'm intelligent . . . I'm intelligent . . . I'm intelligent . . . I'm intelligent . . . I'm intelligent"
Write down what you feel and sense: _____

Now say:
"I'm stupid . . . I'm stupid . . . I'm stupid . . . I'm stupid . . . I'm stupid"
Write down what you feel and sense: _____

Now say:
"I'm happy . . . I'm happy . . . I'm happy . . . I'm happy . . . I'm happy"
Write down what you feel and sense: _____

Now say:
"I'm down . . . I'm down . . . I'm down . . . I'm down . . . I'm down"
Write down what you feel and sense: _____

Now say:

"I can . . . I can . . . I can . . . I can . . . I can"

Write down what you feel and sense: _____

Now say:

"I can't . . . I can't . . . I can't . . . I can't . . . I can't"

Write down what you feel and sense: _____

What feelings and/or sensations did you notice within yourself as you repeated each word? What will you take from this exercise?

Mindful awareness helps us to direct our thoughts, thus giving us greater influence over regulating our emotions and managing our stress and wellness. Good sleep, exercise, and nutrition are basic to feeling better, but learning to change how we think is paramount. The simple fact is: Happy people tend to focus more on the positive side of things! What we know about the plasticity of our ever-growing brain is that with time, intention, and practice, minding our mind helps change the structures of our brain.

Window 4: Your Emotions

Emotions can be powerful and preoccupying. They can drive us in directions that are healthful or not healthful, balanced or unbalanced. Staying and stewing in negative, painful emotions can color your whole view of yourself and your world.

Can you list seven emotions you might have in a single day? What emotions are you aware of right now? Can you name them? In many ways, being aware of your emotions is as important as being aware of your thoughts. As with thoughts, observing and acknowledging your emotions in the present moment from a nonreactive mental space is a key exercise in mindfulness practice. As we have seen, when you cultivate an observing, accepting, calm state of mind, you can change your brain structure and how it functions. Practicing awareness of your emotions can lead to increased emotional regulation, which promotes and fosters resilience in you and the children in your care.

As you allow yourself to become aware of your emotions, you will be better able to recognize the ones you are feeling in any given moment. You can then notice whether they are linked to some identifiable past event or to the present situation. You can do this by asking yourself the following questions:

1. Do these emotions correspond to the truth or reality of what's happening now?
2. Are the emotions I am experiencing helpful?
3. Are they telling me the truth about myself or another person?
4. Do their quality and intensity correspond accurately to the circumstances?
5. Are they supportive, helpful, and proportionate to the situation?

Being the Observer of your emotions means you don't cling to your emotions or push them away. You simply allow them to do what they do; you allow them to move within and through you like waves that roll onto the shore and wash back out into the ocean.

EXERCISE

Again, contemplate the grocery store scenario mentioned earlier. This time sit back and allow yourself to become aware of the emotions that arise within you.

You are about to "lose your cool" because your child is suddenly throwing a major tantrum during a grocery store's rush hour.

You've seen your child do this before, and you know this can trigger a host of negative feelings and negative reactions in you and others.

You are afraid that some critical, disapproving grandmother is about to turn her cart right into your aisle and give you the evil eye for not being a good mother. It doesn't help in the least that Ben and Jerry are also in your shopping basket "melting down" with your child.

You hate looking like a bad parent with a problem child. You want this to stop, and the pressure is on.

Use words to identify particular emotions such as hurt, anger, shame, overwhelm, guilt, fear, and indifference.

Q: What emotional reactions might other shoppers have as they come upon the scene?

1.

2.

Q: If you were watching another parent with a tantrum-throwing child in the grocery store, what might you feel?

1.

2.

Q: If this were you, what feelings would you likely have about yourself?

1.

2.

Q: If this were you, how might you be feeling toward your child?

1.

2.

The benefits of becoming more emotionally aware

Awareness of our emotions arms us with the ability to use our emotions in effective ways, such as crying when we are sad and empowering us when we are feeling victimized. Awareness allows us the opportunity to manage our emotions when we most need to, such as when we are frustrated with our child, angry with our partner, or afraid of our boss. Emotions make life richer and more difficult. Either way, being aware and present to them has many benefits. Here are a few.

- When you are in present awareness with good feelings—such as love, joy, and peacefulness—you can experience them more deeply. (Paying attention to them, they are amplified in your experience.)

- Awareness of your emotional world provides you with more conscious choices, and such choices can translate into better self-control. You can use your mind to disrupt or short circuit toxic or destructive emotions you observe—*before* sparks begin to fly and things are said and done that you may regret later.
- The more effective your own emotional regulation in the course of daily life, the more likely your child will be able to develop emotional balance, including greater capacities for optimism and resilience.

The problems of being emotionally unaware

Have you ever screeched at your child over something simple, such as a glass of spilled milk? Has a bit of rudeness by a teen or preteen ever rubbed you the wrong way and left you sputtering with rage? When we are unclear about what we are feeling and why we are feeling it, we're more likely to be in a reactive, unbalanced state—one that more readily leads to impromptu "knee-jerk" reactions to normal everyday occurrences, such as empty cereal bowls under the bed, a ripped pair of jeans, a lost cell phone, or another argument over who gets to "ride shotgun." Problems occur when we are not aware and in control of our emotions:

- Remorse, guilt, and shame are incurred from something said or done as a result of your automatic reaction.
- Persistent confusion, anxiety, depression, anger, or helplessness within yourself will have a direct impact on your children's states of mind, regulation of emotions, and ability to feel safe.
- Automatic reactions of anger, rage, and frustration

stimulate and reinforce your own tendencies to hyperarousal, thus making it difficult, if not impossible, to stop yourself.

Most parents can easily recall times when they felt out of control. Such memories can be laden with feelings of humiliation, guilt, or self-loathing. As parents, most of us know the feeling of being startled by the strength of such unbalanced reactions. When we feel out of control, our confidence as parents can be shaken. Worse, when we come back to a more emotionally balanced state, we can find ourselves standing in the aftermath of a child's own hurt, fear, and shame.

At such times we often do not know what to do or how to make everything better. We certainly can't promise it will never happen again; nor can we heal the hurt by compensating with gifts or by letting our children have whatever they want for the next few days. Such emotional Band Aids might help *you* feel better in the short term, but they will not repair the loss of connection your children feel each time you lose emotional control in your relationship with them.

Mindfulness and emotional reactivity
What you *can* do is be mindful of your emotional reactivity throughout the day by purposefully attending to the feelings stimulated by certain thoughts or events. Try to be present with the emotions as they arise, and identify if you are:

- *being triggered by an emotional or traumatic event from your past*
- *displacing unresolved feelings about another person or situation onto your child*

Did You Know

Memories become much more powerful when strong emotions are attached to an event. Do you remember where you were, even what you were wearing, when you got the news about two planes crashing in to The World Trade Center on 9/11?

- *experiencing a level and type of emotion appropriate to the current event*

You can use the following questions and scale system to help you reach a clearer understanding of how and what you are doing when you find yourself being reactive in ways that are hurtful or not helpful to yourself or your child:

On a scale of 0-5 (0 being in emotional control and 5 being out of emotional control), what level do I give myself in relationship to this current event?

1. I am a _____ when my child won't listen to me.
2. I am a _____ when my child wants to be with her friends more than with me.
3. I am a _____ when I have to keep asking my children to do their chores.
4. I am a _____ when my children fight with each other.
5. I am a _____ when I didn't get enough sleep or when I am hungry.
6. I am a _____ when my child is grumpy in the morning and we are late.
7. I am a _____ when my children refuse to eat their dinner.

Now it is your turn to create examples from your own situations.

1. I am a _____ when_____.
2. I am a _____ when_____.
3. I am a _____ when_____.
4. I am a _____ when_____.
5. I am a _____ when_____.
6. I am a _____ when_____.
7. I am a _____ when_____.

There are many possible ways to constructively work through strong emotional reactions. For example, consider the following:

⇒ *Talk:* Choose a close friend to talk to. You will want this friend to be the kind that can be empathic, help you check how realistic you are being, and discourage you from wallowing in negative emotions.

⇒ *Meditate*: Sit with the emotion; breathe deeply and slowly while noticing your internal experience without judgment. Remind yourself, *"These feelings are neither good nor bad; they are just feelings."*

⇒ *Write*: Write down five different ways of looking at something. Finding a new way of looking at the situation often helps you come up with a solution to the problem.

⇒ *See a therapist*: If the emotions are causing other symptoms—such as flashbacks, forgetfulness, or feelings of depression, aggression or dissociation—consider talking with a therapist.

As you learn to use such skills to check in with and work through your emotions, eventually you will be better able to identify and make sense of why you feel the way you do. You will get better at interrupting negative emotional reactions, and you will begin to *choose* to focus on associations that carry more positive feelings for you. Doing such things in the course of your day will help you stay connected with yourself and have more emotionally balanced interactions with your child.

Who do you get angry like?
Have you ever asked someone, "Hey, is anything bothering you?" and they responded with a curt "No!" or a sheepish "Everything … is …fine … (sigh)."

In your family of origin, was it okay to express strong emotions, or did you have to stuff them and pretend they weren't there? Were straightforward expressions of anger encouraged and accepted, or did anger tend to come out indirectly, for example, in the slamming of doors or extended periods of icy silence?

Children learn how to manage their emotions from their parents and primary caregivers. While we were growing up, many of us learned that some feelings were okay to talk about and others were not. Likely, we also learned that it was okay to talk about our emotions with certain adults but that others would shrink back or display distress when we tried to tell them how we really felt. Every family has rules about the expression of feelings; sometimes they are conscious and spoken rules; sometimes they are unconscious and implicit. The problem is that no matter how hard we try, it seems impossible to keep from absorbing some of these rules. The rules that governed emotional expression in your family of origin will likely influence your parenting.

The Window of Awareness to your emotions will help you:

- identify what you are feeling and why
- manage your emotions more intentionally
- recognize and acknowledge those emotions or manners of expression that could negatively impact the parent-child connection

In failing to accomplish the above, here are some responses a parent might notice him- or herself having. Some of these statements may even sound familiar from your own childhood:

While growing up, many of us learned that some feelings were okay to talk about and others were not.

- *"Why are you being a big baby? There is nothing to be afraid of."*
- *"I can't believe you are being so sensitive about this!"*
- *"Now be a big boy (or girl), and don't cry. You don't want everyone teasing you, do you?"*

When children are exposed to responses such as these repeatedly, they will more likely than not have difficulty consciously accessing and/or articulating their own emotions in their relationships with others.

The most loving parents will, at times, have difficulty dealing with their child's emotions. Parents raised in families in which emotions were viewed negatively can find themselves being more highly reactive and/or emotionally cut off in their relationships with their children. When a child does have an emotional outburst, or even a small upset, parents who are uncomfortable with emotions may inadvertently deny or suppress their child's feelings in order to reduce their own discomfort. We teach a child to "stuff" his or her emotions by:

- minimizing how the child feels
- rationalizing emotions to make them seem unimportant or less relevant
- intellectualizing emotional experience, thereby effectively distancing the child from the real experience of his or her emotions
- bargaining with bribes or rewards to encourage a child's repression or rejection of his or her emotions
- distracting children with food, TV, toys, and other things that can effectively numb them emotionally or distance them from how they are feeling

Such tactics have potentially negative and long-lasting consequences in the development of a child's healthy regulatory emotional system. When parents can be comfortable with their own emotions, they are more capable of accepting and tolerating their child's as well. When parents are in circumstances where a child is expressing strong emotions, it is important for them to remember that children learn how to regulate their emotions more effectively by experiencing them to begin with.

When parents can be comfortable with their own emotions, they are more capable of accepting and tolerating their child's as well.

EXERCISE

Consider and note the family rule that might govern each of the following questions or statements. Then—assuming each statement was made by a parent to a child—write down how you imagine the parent who said these things might have felt as they spoke them.

1. *"Why are you being a big baby? There is nothing to be afraid of."*

   Rule: _____

   Parent's emotion behind the statement: _____

   _____

2.   *"I can't believe you are being so sensitive about this!"*

Rule: _____

Parent's emotion behind the statement: _____

_____

3.   *"Be a big boy (or girl), and don't cry. You don't want anyone teasing you, do you?"*

Rule: _____

Parent's emotion behind the statement: _____

_____

What you wrote may well be true, and here are some other possibilities:

1.   Rule: *Being afraid is not okay.*
     Parent: *"I feel guilty that I can't always protect you from being afraid."*

2.   Rule: *Being sensitive shows weakness.*
     Parent: *"I am afraid my child will be picked on."*

3.   Rule: *Crying is for cowards.*
     Parent: *"I am embarrassed; I don't know what to do."*

Let's go back to the family *genogram* I discussed in chapter 1. When I am working with new clients, I look at their family patterns by drawing a family genogram. I explore the "unspoken rules" their family lives by in the universe of emotions. Are feelings accepted or avoided? Are they talked through? Are they denied? As you look through the window into your emotional world, understanding what conscious or unconscious rules you live by helps your children navigate their internal worlds of emotion. Being attuned to your emotions is the only way to be deeply attuned to your children's.

Through mindfulness practice, you can become more attuned and comfortable with your own emotions. Moreover, you can develop a more sensitive antenna to help you remain in touch with your feelings and be more connected to yourself in important ways. You will be better prepared to recognize that your feelings are always changing and to manage them into a balanced state.

Likewise, remember that being aware of and observing your emotions will allow you to make choices that will help your child feel more connected to you. Your child can be only as emotionally connected with you as you are with yourself.

Window 5: Your Interconnectedness

Do you ever sense the emotions being experienced by another? When someone passes by and smiles at you, do you feel more upbeat? Have you been to a wedding where you don't know the tearful bride, but as she passes down the aisle, you find yourself becoming teary-eyed too? When you watch a baby reach another milestone—like standing for the first time—do you register his or her feeling of astonishment? At such times, you are looking at yourself and life through the Window of Interconnectedness. In this win-

As you begin to understand your feelings, you develop greater compassion toward yourself, which promotes the development of greater empathy and attunement with your child.

dow you can see and experience the myriad connections in and through which we live.

Throughout history sages, scientists, and scholars have recognized how everything is interconnected. As our body of knowledge and technological prowess increase, our survival will be increasingly dependent on how well we consciously manage the interdependent systems that support, inform, and enhance life on this planet.

As we have seen, how you connect with yourself serves as a primary foundation for your child's developing sense of self and general orientation to life. Developing the Windows of Awareness enables you to connect with *you* while you effectively manage the flow of energy and information within your brain and body that, if left unchecked, yields reactions that negatively impact us and the world around us.

By paying attention to the 5th Window of Awareness, we extend awareness beyond "self-ness" to include awareness of our "we-ness." This practice will help you boost some of the more crucial capacities necessary for a high-quality, healthy parent-child connection, including *Attunement and Empathy*.

> *"When one tugs at a single thing in Nature, he finds it attached to the rest of the world"*
> –John Muir

What connects you and me?
Have you ever wondered why seeing someone yawn makes you want to yawn too? We now know that this reaction is stimulated by *mirror neurons* in your brain. These specialized nerve cells are largely responsible for what makes us so-

cial creatures. They are largely responsible for why we can rightly call the brain the "social organ" of the human body. Mirror neurons enable us to experience within ourselves the internal states and actions of other people … as they are occurring. When you see someone yawn, the mirror neurons in your brain are triggered, and you respond in kind. When you smile at your child, this triggers activation of the same mirror neurons in your child. When you laugh, your child will be inclined to laugh. The same rule goes with frowning, by the way! When you give positive attention to your child, your child will be more likely to feel an internal positive response and be more likely to express that internal response outwardly.

"We are exquisitely social creatures. Our survival depends on understanding the actions, intentions, and emotions of others. Mirror neurons allow us to grasp the minds of others not through conceptual reasoning but through direct simulation. By feeling, not by thinking."
–Giaocomo Rizzolatti

Mirror neurons carry out their orders in specific areas of our brain, which include the following: our premotor cortex, our center for language, our center for pain, and our center for empathy. Neuroscientists have found that mirror neurons are the mechanisms that give us a *mental experience* when we watch someone do something, whether it is yawning, laughing, crying, or licking an ice cream cone. When we watch the actions of others, our mirror neurons are not only "mimicking" the action, but they also are enabling us to understand and feel the intention or meaning behind the action. When we smile at a child, her mirror neurons return the action, and this reinforces learning about smiling as well the felt meaning that goes with the smile. These fantastic mirror neurons play a fundamental role in our sense of interpersonal connectedness. They provide the mechanism that makes it possible for us to attune and empathize with others to a profound degree.

For a wonderful dramatization of how our connections with one another—including complete strangers—make it possible for an emotional response to spread from one person to another, stop and take a few minutes to watch a video on YouTube.com called *Bodhisattva in metro* (2009).

The story begins with everyday people riding on the metro. The passengers are keeping to themselves, detached from each other's worries, sorrows, and joys. Some people are reading; most appear resigned—just another day on the metro. At one of the stops a man gets on the train and sits down. He looks happy, and there is a mischievous smirk on his face. As the train begins to move, he snickers. His snickers percolate into chuckles. His chuckles soon explode into uncontrollable laughter. Fellow passengers look up or turn to see where the laughter is coming from. Some respond immediately with expressions of curiosity or amusement. Others seem anxious and uncertain. The man continues to laugh until he is roaring, rocking back and forth in his seat. A few passengers begin to smile. Some of the passengers try to repress their initial reaction, but the tide of laughter ultimately proves irresistible. Their smiles become chuckles, and their chuckling quickly turns into laughter. The contagion spreads like wildfire until ev-

These fantastic mirror neurons play a fundamental role in our sense of interpersonal connectedness.

eryone in the train car is rocking back and forth with laughter. Faces are red, bodies are jiggling, and eyes are streaming. These people are laughing for real. When the train comes to a stop, the laughter dies down to a low hum. As new passengers enter the car and find their place, everyone tries to hold back their laughter. Then one person can't hold it back any longer and lets out a loud hoot, and everyone combusts into another round of uncontrolled laughter.

Each time I watch this video I can't help but laugh along with the passengers. I experience tickles in my stomach and warmth in my face. My laughter is not a response to any joke, funny dialogue, or pratfall. In fact, not a single word is spoken throughout the video. Even so, as I laugh, I feel connected to them. If I were to catch a reflection of myself while watching this video, I am certain I would look very much like the passengers I am watching and listening to: squinting eyes, open mouth, pink cheeks, and shaking body. My mirror neurons certainly take delight in watching this video!

As you parent, keep in mind the knowledge of how mirror neurons work, and then positively influence the cultivation and integration of your child's internal mental and emotional states.

By practicing being in a resonant, attuned state with your own mental world, you can become more capable of achieving it with another.

Delving Deeper: Marvelous Mirror Neurons

When you get stabbed with a needle, neurons in your brain's anterior cingulate are triggered. Surprisingly, researchers have discovered that the same neurons will fire when you watch someone else being stabbed [1]! But there is more. This sympathetic mirroring effect—attributed to other brain cells called "mirror neurons"—is also evident as we watch someone else perform a variety of specific tasks or movements [2].

These mirror neurons enable us to experience reality from another person's perspective and contribute significantly to our capacities for learning through observation and imitation. They give us the capacity to feel what another is feeling, grasp what another is thinking, and anticipate the intended actions of another. Some propose that they are instrumental in the learning of language. Ultimately, they enable the human organism to adapt collectively and participate in the development and maintenance of culture [3].

Given how it functions, the mirror neuron system (MNS) is indispensible in processes of human development. When a child's MNS is exposed to caregiver behavior that is straightforward and congruent, he or she is able to "map" the mental and emotional states, intentions, and actions of others with more confidence and accuracy. On the other hand, if caregivers act in confusing ways or are difficult to "read," the child's interpretations of social experience are more vulnerable to distortion and insecurity.

YOU developing attunement

Likely, you are familiar with the pleasure that comes with feeling close to another person. Such feelings are the hallmark of *attunement*, which can be characterized as a kind of sympathetic resonance with the internal world of another person.

Our mirror neurons make it possible for us to sense another person's inner experience and intentions. To some degree and at various times, this felt sense of attunement is naturally available to most of us, but it can be cultivated, strengthened, and made more consistent through mindfulness practice. By practicing being in a resonant, attuned state with your own mental world, you can become more capable of achieving it with another.

A *Star Trek* Fan might try to identify attunement with what the fictional characters from the planet Vulcan call "mind melding," but this isn't quite accurate. Attunement is not a telepathic link to a shared lived-experience of the thoughts, feelings, and memories of another. In the context of mindful parenting, however, it can be understood as an immediate *felt sense* of what your child is experiencing, wanting, or needing at a given moment.

When you tune in and pay attention to your child, you can learn to read and interpret more accurately the signals your child uses to tell you what he or she wants. For example, imagine that your preverbal infant pulls on his cheek and begins to whimper when he is hungry. As you take in these signals, your mirror neurons are activated in the same area of your brain, and—unless you are distracted or in some other way mentally blocking or filtering the signals—you experience within yourself what your child's experience may be like. This social mechanism helps you translate the meaning behind your child's signals, thereby helping to ensure that you respond appropriately.

As you get to know your child, you are encoding the needs, wants, and intentions behind his or her behaviors. This helps establish a responsive communication link between the two of you. To someone not as close to you or your child, the meaning of a child's signals will not be as clear as they are to you. You, on the other hand, will learn through being attuned and by responding to the likely meaning behind a child's particular sounds, gestures, expressions, and other behaviors.

Did You Know

You can influence the structures and functions of your brain. If you want to be more patient, you can use your intention to help develop new neural pathways that will help you become more patient. It takes a lot of practice, so be patient!

"My children know I love them. Interestingly, it seemed so much more meaningful when I acknowledge their love for me. Their energy and facial expressions let me know this!"
—Mallory, A Mindful Mom

Now that you have learned about mirror neurons, you can see why it is so important to be attuned with yourself and with your child. Your children have mirror neurons too. They are observing and encoding everything you do—how you feel internally when you are happily flowing through life, or when you are stressed, hurt, angry, afraid, or rejecting. Your nonverbal signals and actions are continually being deciphered and stimulating reactions in your child's brain and central nervous system. Being a mindful parent keeps this question in the forefront of your mind: *What "felt-sense" of me do I want my children to have?*

Attunement promotes secure attachment
Most of us intuitively understand that a person with a secure style of attachment had parents or caregivers who were attuned to them and responsive to them when they were children. The adults in their lives recognized the communication signals they used to express particular needs. The primary caretakers were able to interpret those signals accurately and respond to them in a timely, caring, and appropriate manner.

At the same time, most of us do not yet understand that responding optimally to the needs of the children in our care requires a dual focus: We must stay attuned to our own internal worlds of sensation, thought, and emotion while we also pay attention to the signals our children use to communicate their needs to us.

If you are too focused on your inner world, you may miss some very important messages your child is trying to send your way, for example, a message regarding some need for comfort and attention.

If you are too focused on your inner world, you may miss some very important messages your child is trying to send your way, for example, a message regarding some need for comfort and attention. Imagine, for example, that you are enjoying a conversation on the phone with a friend while, in the next room and unbeknown to you, your daughter is creating a work of art on the wall with crayons. It may be that prior to connecting with your friend on the phone, your child had been signaling that she needed some attention, but you had somehow missed the message. Perhaps you had returned from the grocery store and were focused on getting things put away, or you were trying to complete a list of chores that were piling up. Either way, your child may have had a feeling that you were unavailable, and experienced frustration over having to compete with others for your attention, which resulted in the unmanaged expressivity that resembled a Picasso.

What might your child learn if this kind of inattention occurs repeatedly? That she is not worth your attention? That she has to take care of her own needs, even though she may not yet be able to express them or know how to meet them? That she has to act out in ways that will more surely get you to respond to her, even if that response is negative? Of course, we don't want or intend for our children to learn such things, but what you want or intend will not be enough to prevent them from learning them.

Attunement is an important key to a better parent-child connection. Through an attuned relationship your children are more likely to feel that you can read their signals and effectively respond to them. This kind of responsiveness keeps the bond between you and your children going and growing.

Use the following exercise to explore some real-life situations and distractions that are likely to hijack your attention away from your child. Use what you discover to reorient yourself and prioritize how you will attend to your own needs and the needs of your child.

EXERCISE

Answer each of the questions. Take time to think about past and recent situations.

1. When I am feeling _____, all I want to do is _____

_____

2. After a long day at work, I want to_____

_____

3. When my child is in a whiney mood, what I think and feel is _____

_____

4. When I am reading or watching TV and my child keeps interrupting me, I feel

_____and respond by _____

_____

5. When my child pulls at my leg while I am trying to get dinner on the table,

I _____

_____

Now, make a list of some of the important signals (e.g., sounds, words, expressions, gestures, and movements) your child uses to communicate with you, and identify the need indicated by each signal. The first one is an example.

The signal is _____ *whiney, rubbing eyes* _____ the need is _____ *a nap* _____

The signal is _____ the need is _____

The signal is _____ the need is _____

The signal is _____ the need is _____

The signal is _____ the need is _____

The signal is _____ the need is _____

The signal is _____ the need is _____

The signal is _____ the need is _____

The signal is _____ the need is _____

The signal is _____ the need is _____

Reflect on your answers and note any insights, ideas, feelings or patterns of reactivity or responsiveness that you have become aware of:

I am more aware of _____

_____

This is a helpful exercise to return to as your child matures. You may find yourself adding to or changing the list of signals your child uses to indicate a need. You can also return to the list from time to time to remind yourself of how you can most effectively respond to your child.

Remember, secure attachment results from a parent or caretaker being:

1. attuned to how a child uses communication signals to express a need
2. able to the read and interpret a child's signals accurately
3. responsive to a child's needs in a timely and caring way

YOU increasing empathy

In addition to attunement, a healthy bond between you and another person requires *empathy*. According to Siegel (2010), empathy is the capacity to have some sense of "the internal mental stance of another person." Empathy can be enhanced through mindfulness practice as well. As we become increasingly capable of becoming aware of, observing, and describing the variety of feelings, thoughts, and reactions that arise within us, the more skillful we are likely to become at comprehending and imagining what it is like to walk in another person's shoes.

"The more we are able to keep in mind the intrinsic wholeness and beauty of our children—especially when it's difficult to see—the more our ability to be mindful deepens."
–Jon Kabat-Zinn

Empathy also contributes to the development of a strong parent-child connection. It provides a shared understanding through which your child can experience a greater sense of closeness and comfort with you.

Healthy empathy does not involve becoming emotionally enmeshed or overly identified with another. A micromanaging, overprotective parent probably needs to work on cultivating a more balanced capacity for empathy. True empathy is not about "fixing" your child; rather, it is about being present with your child in a way that communicates you really "get it"—that you understand how it feels when someone breaks up with you, or what it's like when you are not invited to the party.

Real empathy requires a significant focus upon the experience of another. Simply being present with yourself as you imagine what your child is experiencing from his or her own point of view can enhance a more secure and stable attachment bond between you and your child.

Real empathy can often be communicated with few words—and sometimes without speaking at all. While some self-disclosure or explanation can enhance the empathic connection in a relationship, too much sharing from your own standpoint can dilute or destroy a child's feeling of being understood.

You can develop your capacities for empathy by taking time during the day to:

- allow yourself to feel how others might be seeing and interpreting their own life circumstances
- imagine and reflect upon the impact of an event you hear about in the news and the people directly involved with it, or the personal impact of circumstances that are being experienced by a friend or family member

Real empathy
can often be
communicated
with few
words—and
sometimes
without speaking
at all.

Take some time to exercise your mirror neurons by responding in writing to the following statements. There is no right or wrong answer. If you find yourself over-thinking or trying to edit your answer, move on to the next question. You can always return to a question later.

1. When I see or imagine a baby bird that has fallen from its nest, I feel _____, and the sensation I experience in my body is_____.

2. When I see or imagine a child getting scolded in public, I feel _____, and I experience _____ in my body.

3. When I see or imagine someone standing while watching his or her home burning down, I feel _____, and I think _____ _____.

4. When I see or imagine my child being teased at school, I feel _____ _____, and I _____.

5. When I see or imagine someone's pet lying dead in the road, I feel _____, and I_____.

6. When I see or imagine yelling at my child, I feel _____and my body is _____.

A purposeful directing of our awareness to the connections we have with ourselves and others is ultimately a matter of choice. Choosing to engage in the mindful development of *attunement* and *empathy* nurtures and fortifies our relationships. As we have seen, such work is especially important in the raising of joyful and resilient children. As we give ourselves opportunities to cultivate inner qualities such as mental calm, nonreactivity, and nonjudgment, we will be adding to our personal health and happiness. This cultivation of self helps strengthen and stabilize the parent-child connection; it is a primary step in the cultivation of more securely attached children.

Make it a daily practice to *see* things as if for the first time, and use your *imagination* to grasp the internal experience of another. Hold their experience close to you, and feel in your heart what it must be like for them. Remember, through mindfulness practice you can do the following:

- Use your mind to change your brain. Your human biology supports your ability to adapt and grow, not only within yourself, but also in your relationships with others. You can improve upon what nature has given you to better nurture your children, family, and community.
- Support relationship growth by extending your awareness beyond your own experience in order to more fully comprehend the interconnected networks in which you live and upon which you depend for survival, meaning, and fulfillment.
- Become attuned and empathic with your children and with their teachers, mentors, neighbors, or caregivers. Affirm these important adults for their hard work on behalf of children. (This is a powerful

As we give ourselves opportunities to cultivate inner qualities such as mental calm, nonreactivity, and nonjudgment, we will be adding to our personal health and happiness.

antidote that helps prevent burnout!)

- Consider who else in your life might benefit from having a few minutes of feeling heard and understood; then go to them with the intention to be attuned and empathic. Really listening—mindfully—is powerful medicine.

Phase 2: Self-Intervention

BACK IN BALANCE: (TINGLE)

Self Intervention

1. **T**imeout for parents
2. **I**nhale-exhale
3. **N**ame it
4. **G**round yourself
5. **L**oosen up
6. **E**valuate your state of mind

In phase 1, by attending to the *Five Windows of Awareness*, you began to observe more thoroughly your sensory experience, your body, your thoughts, your feelings, and your connections between yourself and the world around you. As you practice such self-observation, you will improve your ability to recognize when you are more or less balanced mentally and emotionally. Moreover, as you pay attention with nonjudgmental acceptance, you will develop and reinforce the quality of self-attunement that is so essential to a healthy parent-child connection.

Phase 2 is about practicing *self-intervention*. Taking specific action to mentally step in and disrupt negative patterns of thought, emotion, and behavior will help you stay, or regain balance. Ideally, you will be able to self-intervene *before* you cross the threshold from feeling in control to feeling out of control. If you cross the line—becoming reactive to the point that you are no longer able to regulate your own thoughts, emotions, and behaviors for the good of yourself and/or your child—hit the "pause" button, breathe, observe, notice what's happening, and then move on to the next steps of self-intervention.

This scenario below is called "Getting out the Door." I will be referring to it throughout this phase and in the Deliberate Action phase as well.

It's 7 A.M. *and you need to get the kids out the door in thirty minutes. You are more stressed than usual because there's a big meeting at work, and you've learned that layoffs are coming. Today happens to be the day when your youngest child refuses to get dressed and your oldest, who didn't sleep well, is slow moving and extremely grumpy. You choose to practice mindfulness, paying attention to yourself and your internal reactions as you gather lunches and keep things moving along. You notice your body is tense, your jaws are clenched, your heart is racing, and your face feels hot. You also observe that you feel afraid that you will be late for work. You try to maintain mental and emotional balance as you talk to your children calmly and directly, but for some reason you feel increasingly tense. Then the dog runs in from the backyard with muddy feet that soil your carpet. Just one more problem or point of stress will trigger you to explode.*

This is an excellent situation for a parent to apply a *self-intervention*. Interrupt your reactivity before the dam breaks or the internal bomb goes off. Such a self-intervention is like pressing your brain's "pause button" in order to give you some time to get back into a balanced state. And just how do you manage to do this? The acronym **TINGLE** can help. Tingle provides a path to maintain and regain a more balanced state.

TINGLE provides you with six sequential steps to take when practicing self-intervention. Take a few minutes to review and memorize them.

Timeout
Inhale-exhale
Name it
Ground yourself
Loosen up
Evaluate your mind

Notice how the TINGLE exercise can help you recover mental and emotional balance so that you can think more carefully and strategically about how you want to approach the situation.

When you want or need to TINGLE, try to give yourself a momentary break from the children by moving into another room or separate space. If your child is likely to become upset when you leave the room, or follow you as you absent yourself, try staying in the room. Sit on the floor holding your child, and concentrate on breathing deeply and slowly. You may notice that as you pay attention to your breathing, your child's own breathing will begin to match yours. (When this happens, it can be an indication that attunement is occurring!) You may find it easier to spend a few quiet moments together as you practice TINGLE-ing.

Such a self-intervention is like pressing your brain's "pause button" in order to give you some time to get back into a balanced state.

Timeout for parents:

A self-intervention begins with the parent recognizing the need to take a timeout. The age of your child or a variety of other circumstances will determine how you take a time-out. There are *mental* timeouts where you stay with your children and practice the TINGLE steps in their presence, and physical timeouts where you assess whether it is safe to remove yourself from the situation. A mental timeout is used when the children are too young for you to remove yourself, or if you are in a situation you can't leave, such as riding in a car. A physical timeout is appropriate only when your children are old enough to be left alone or will be safe with someone else present, like an older sibling or adult.

A timeout can be for five minutes or an hour, but the parent is the one who initiates it, and if needed, the one to remove him- or herself to another room. If you need a mental timeout, shift your focus from the external world to your internal world. As you apply the TINGLE steps, adjust them so that you can remain with your children. If you are able to take a physical timeout, calmly tell your children that you need a few minutes to yourself.

There are three rules to delivering physical timeouts:
1. you must tell your children where you will be
2. you must tell them what time you will be back
3. you must give them the parameters

When announcing the timeout, speak to them calmly and firmly. You will be more convincing if you have a well-rehearsed "oneliner" you have practiced in preparation for such moments, such as: *"Mommy needs a timeout to settle down and take care of herself so that she can take better care of you. I am going to be in my room for ten minutes. During this time you get 'free time' to do any one of these things."* Pick enjoyable activities such as watching TV or playing a game. Then remove yourself from the room.

> *"Shallow breathing is a symptom of an anxious mind."*
> –Sam Keen

I*nhale-exhale:*
Begin your timeout by focusing on your breath. Close your eyes so you are better able to pay attention to the experience of breathing in and out. If your mind wanders, notice it and describe it to yourself (wandering), then gently return your attention to your breath. Intentionally slow your breathing down and make it deeper. Breathing in this way sends more oxygen to your brain and helps your system slow down. You can invite compassion and kindness with each inhalation and exhalation; for example, *"I breathe in love, I exhale love"* or *"I breathe in my goodness, I exhale my goodness."* Mindful breathing can help you restore your own sense of safety and stability. Adding a mantra of compassion and kindness can activate self-empathy.

N*ame it:*
Now that you are breathing calmly and thinking clearly again, it is time to make sense of what's happening and gain some new perspective. It's time to ask yourself a few introspective questions:

1. What is it that has stirred me up so much?
2. What am I feeling? On a scale of 0-5, where 5 is the most aroused, what number best represents my current level of emotional intensity?
3. What am I worried about? Am I being pessimistic

or dwelling too much on the worst-case scenario?

4. Is my reaction related to something in my past?
5. How much of my response has to do with my child's stress versus my own?

Now, describe what you are experiencing right now. Relative to the scene above, a parent's response might be something like one or more of the following:

"I am stirred up because we are going to be late if my children don't begin to cooperate and get with my plan."

"I am feeling frustrated and overwhelmed."

"I am worried that my children will be late to school and the teachers will think I am irresponsible. I am also afraid I will end up being late to work, which will jeopardize my good standing with the company."

"My parents always told me, 'If you do things right, you will be successful; if you do things wrong, you will pay a price.'"

"Both my children are having a difficult morning; maybe it is because they stayed up past their bedtime last night. I am also having a difficult morning, and I think my children are picking up on this."

Target and summarize the salient issues. This will help you be more immediately present to yourself and to your circumstances, which will provide you a better mental starting place from which you will be better prepared to move forward.

"My kids and I are having a tough morning. If I give us room to be a little late, I will be calmer and more attentive to my children's individual difficulties. I can call my boss to inform her/ him that I will be running a little late."

Ground yourself:

It is much more difficult to achieve mental and emotional balance when you are harshly self-critical, negatively judging others, or discounting yourself because of the situation. Having and holding on to negative judgments only hurts you and your child. Judgments close the blinds on seeing things from another's point of view. Judgment does not promote compassion. Our perceptions stay narrow, and our ability to open our hearts with compassion becomes constrictive.

Removing or neutralizing such judgments through self-awareness, observation, and self-acceptance can free up your energy and attention for more beneficial and constructive uses. When you observe the critical voice of judgment, whether it is toward yourself or your child, it is a good time to close your eyes, put the palm of your hands over your heart, and focus on compassion, forgiveness, and gentle kindness. Ask yourself how you would want to be treated in this situation, and let the answer come to your mind from your heart. If you take a few moments to ground yourself in compassion you will be better able to be deliberate in your actions.

Loosen up:

Next, take a moment to shake it loose—literally. Turn on some music, sing out loud, and shake, wiggle, walk, or do jumping jacks. You have just experienced a surge of adren-

Judgments close the blinds on seeing things from another's point of view.

alin in your bloodstream; now you need to release some energy from your body so that you can give yourself an opportunity to be more relaxed. This is a good time to perform a quick body scan. Observe any area in which you might be holding tension. Move your jaw around, shake your hands, shimmy your shoulders. Loosening up your body will help you loosen up your mind. See if you are able to look at the situation from another perspective. Try to find the funny or the important lesson this situation offers.

Evaluate your mind:
Now take a moment to observe yourself again. (Remember: The more centered you are within yourself, the more balanced and attuned you can be with your child—no matter what the situation.) Use the following questions to help you determine if you are ready to move on to the model's third and final phase: *Deliberate Action.*

- Am I able to think clearly?
- Has my level of emotional arousal (using the 0-5 scale) decreased?
- Is my body settled down and relaxed?
- Can I think creatively?
- Can I express words and actions that model love and leadership?
- Can I find a solution that teaches my child something about life?

If you can answer yes to these questions, you are prepared to move on to *the next phase, Deliberate Action.*

Self-Intervention is the bridge you must cross in order to think more rationally, regulate your emotions, and assess your goals. Self-intervention takes your brain out of overdrive. Your amygdala—which fuels and modulates re-active responses—cools down, and your prefrontal cortex reasserts its executive functions. From this calmer mental space, you can more effectively evaluate the circumstances in which you find yourself.

Now that your attention is in the present moment and you have interrupted negative thoughts, emotions, and behaviors, continue maintaining internal awareness. Consciously continue to slow your pace of breathing and make it deeper. Observe and name the different aspects of your experience as you become aware of them. As you become grounded in the present through awareness and self-intervention, you will enable yourself to move into a more balanced, self-attuned state.

Phase 3: Deliberate Action

RESPONDING WITH INTENTION: DEVISING A PLAN

Deliberate Action

1. Create a goal
2. Devise a strategy
3. Join with your child
4. Identify life-skills to teach
5. Lead with lightness

The third and final phase, Deliberate Action, is concerned with the plan you make that keeps the parent-child connection going while you are interacting with your child. It doesn't matter if you are teaching your children to recognize or set limits, or trying to get them to do their homework. In this phase your planned interaction includes keeping your children feeling safe, secure, respected and heard.

As you experience more calm and stability within yourself, consider your values and what is most important to you. If you are interacting with your child, think about your child's point of view; feel "into" what he or she might be experiencing internally; and imagine responding intentionally, with flexibility and creativity.

You are preparing for *Deliberate Action*. In the *Deliberate Action* phase don't become preoccupied with what happened in the past. Rather, plan the sequence of steps you want to take as you work things through. Remember, whatever plan you come up with, the purpose for the overall goal is the same: to respond in a way that will support a secure and stable parent-child connection.

Devising a Plan of Action

Devising a plan of action is a dress rehearsal for how you want to be when you reunite with your child so that you can successfully work through whatever caused you to step back from the situation. The following steps can help you take deliberate action that will maintain and strengthen the connection you have with your child.

> Step 1: Create a goal. Answer the question, *"What do I want to achieve here?"*
>
> Step 2: Devise a strategy. Answer the question, *"How can I be effective in helping my child follow my lead?"*
>
> Step 3: Join with your child. Develop a plan of action that involves empathy and a level of shared effort with your child that is appropriate to her or his age and maturity.

What is my goal?

What is my

strategy?

How can I join

with my children?

Which life skills do

I want to teach?

How can I keep it

light and still lead?

Step 4: Teach life skills using the following action sequence:

- Identify the skills you want your child to learn.
- Model the life skills you want to teach.
- Reinforce the skills you see your child pick-up on.

Step 5: Keep it light. Inasmuch as possible, approach deliberate action as a way to shift the mood. When a parent needs to do a self-intervention, it is usually due to a pretty heated or potentially heated situation. Remember, when you go back to re-engage with your child, you are teaching him or her new skills. They will learn better if they feel safe and close to you. Keeping it light shows control over a situation while still setting boundaries and exerting parental leadership … without shaming or being punitive. You are teaching that conflict is natural, but it also requires resolutions and cooperation.

Putting It into Action

Now let's return to the "Getting out the Door" scenario. Here is how this parent planned her five steps:

1. What is my goal?
   - *My goal is to get my children to school in positive moods so they can have a good day.*
2. What is my strategy?
   - *First, I will shift the mood in the house. I need to be less anxious and tense. I will turn on some of the kids' favorite music and play it loudly. I will begin to bring my kids into a dance. I will laugh, I will sing, and I will be playful.*

- *Once they are giggling, I will keep them dancing. I will get my younger child's school clothes, and while she is dancing, I will dress her. To help out my older child, I will do a few of the tasks he has not yet completed.*
- *While holding my younger child's hand, I will then ask my older child to turn the music down.*

3. How can I join with my children in making this a shared effort?
   - *When the music is turned down, I will bring the kids into a huddle with an, "Okay team SMITH! This team is the best at pulling together. Here's what were going to do."*
   - *I will turn to my oldest and ask him what he still needs to get done before leaving the house. I will then ask the same of my youngest. When they tell me, I will pretend I am setting a timer and frame these activities as a race to see who can accomplish their tasks and get back to "THIS SAME SPOT" before a certain time.*

(Believe it or not this can all be done in five minutes!)

4. What life-skills will I be teaching my children?
   - *I want my children to learn a few things from me: 1) I want them to learn how to shift and manage their moods; 2) I want them to see me as a leader and follow my direction; 3) I want them to make decisions based on outcome, even if it is as simple as who's going to "win the race;" and 4) I want to teach them that they may not want to go to school or get dressed, but we need to do things we don't want to sometimes. This is life.*

Did You Know

Life skills provide the tools children need to have satisfying relationships and live up to their potential. They include academic competency, verbal and non-verbal communication skills, problem solving, planning ahead, ability to receive criticism and rejection, personal care, and money management.

In other words, the parent in this situation is now able to envision her children being exposed to a wonderful set of important life skills:

- adapting to change
- following direction
- making decisions based on a desired outcome
- thinking and feeling more positively
- putting aside what we feel like doing in order to do what must get done (impulse control and delayed gratification)

5. How will I keep it light?

- *I will influence the children's moods by doing the following: shifting my mood, turning on music I know they will enjoy, playfully initiating dancing and singing, making a team huddle, and turning the remaining tasks into a game. As we do these different things, we can feel "lighter." We will be more likely to get out of our drudgery and rut and into action. This will also improve the likelihood that the children will arrive at school in better moods, more ready to learn, and feeling more connected with me throughout the day. If just some of this gets accomplished, I know I will be in a better mood for the other work I have to do today.*

As you encounter opportunities to practice mindful parenting throughout your day, use the five steps of *Deliberate Action* to develop your own strategic plan. It will also be helpful to look at past situations, go through the same steps, and devise a plan for them. The more you think out scenarios by answering the questions, the easier it will be to come up with positive actions when you are in the "heat of the moment." Thinking and planning ahead will make it more likely that you will be able to follow through with your intention. This is much like the information a fire chief told an audience: *"You have a higher chance of survival if you have thought out a plan of action ahead of time, should you find yourself in a situation where a fire breaks out."*

I have been in such a situation. I was living in a historical building with shake shingles that was surrounded by a canyon of eucalyptus trees and brush. The city I live in has a "fire season." After listening to the advice of the fire chief, I made a mental plan of what I would grab first if I needed to leave immediately. One fall day I heard the familiar voice of a neighbor yelling *"Fire."* I didn't panic or question what I should do; rather, I robotically responded exactly as I had planned. I continue to create mental plans like this. I look for exits in populated situations. When I am walking alone, I plan what I will do if a stranger approaches me. When I am driving, I make plans to respond when other people cut me off or suddenly stop in front of me.

As you can see, *Deliberate Action* extends beyond parenting to actual survival. With practice you will find it easier to mentally plan for deliberate action without having to write your ideas down, but for now, writing the answers to the questions presented here will help you think sequentially and respond effectively.

Using the Model: Some Final Notes

When the parents I work with are first introduced to the three-phase model, some have difficulty believing that they have the time necessary to apply it. Others find it difficult to imagine excusing themselves from their children for a few minutes to work through the model and create a plan for deliberate action.

By now it should be apparent that cultivating mindfulness is, in the first instance, not about having a quick fix to an immediate problem. A mindful parent has much to be aware of and informed about. Mindful parenting involves ongoing practice and resolve.

Make every effort to *give yourself mindfulness breaks*. You are not abandoning your children when you explain to them that you need a few minutes to yourself. Instead, you are giving your child an opportunity to learn:

1. Each of us needs some personal time and space to take care of ourselves so that we are able to meet the responsibilities and demands of life more effectively.

2. Healthy mental and emotional self-regulation helps us establish and maintain good boundaries between ourselves and others.

3. Cultivating a better connection with self is an indispensible part of building better relationships with others.

In the next chapter you will find additional exercises—based on mindful awareness, self-intervention, and deliberate action—to help you continue developing as a mindful parent. Keep up the good work!

Quick Glance: Chapter Four

⇒ The Mindful Parent Happy Child Model
   Mindful Awareness
   Self-Intervention
   Deliberate Action

⇒ The model is designed to help you apply principles of mindfulness in the context of your everyday interactions with your child in order to strengthen the *parent-child connection*.

Phase 1: Mindful Awareness

⇒ The Five Windows of Awareness
   Developing your mindful parenting practice involves attending to five different areas of your "whole" self, which I refer to as the Five Windows:
   1. your five senses (*taste, touch, sound, sight, and smell*)
   2. your body (*your physical self and its sensations*)
   3. your thoughts (*perceptions, beliefs, assumptions, and judgments*)
   4. your emotions (*including hurt, anger, shame, fear, loneliness, guilt, comfort, peace, happiness, and joy*)
   5. your interconnections with others (*especially your experiences of developing and sharing an attuned state with another person*)

Phase 2: Self-Intervention

⇒ Phase 2 is about practicing *self-intervention*. Taking specific action to mentally step in and disrupt negative patterns of thought, emotion, and behavior will help you stay, or regain more balanced.

⇒ If you cross the line—becoming reactive to the point that you are no longer able to regulate your own thoughts, emotions, and behaviors for the good of yourself and/or your child—hit the "pause" button, breathe, observe, notice what's happening, and then move on to the next steps of self-intervention.

⇒ **TINGLE** provides you with six sequential steps to take when practicing self-intervention. Take a few minutes to review and memorize them.

Timeout for parents
Inhale-exhale
Name it
Ground yourself
Loosen up
Evaluate your state of mind

⇒ *Self-Intervention* is the bridge you must cross in order to think more rationally, regulate your emotions, and assess your goals. Self-intervention takes your brain out of overdrive.

Phase 3: Deliberate Action

⇒ As you experience more calm and stability within yourself, consider your values and what is most important to you. If you are interacting with your child, think about your child's point of view; feel "into" what he or she might be experiencing internally; and imagine responding intentionally, with flexibility and creativity.

⇒ Devising a Plan
Step 1: Create a goal. Answer the question, *"What do I want to achieve here?"*

Step 2: Devise a strategy. Answer the question, *"How can I be effective in helping my child follow my lead?"*

Step 3: Join with your child. Develop a plan of action that involves empathy and a level of shared effort with your child that is appropriate to her or his age and maturity.

Step 4: Teach life skills using the following action sequence:
- Identify the skills you want your child to learn.
- Model the life skills you want to teach.
- Reinforce the skills you see your child pick-up on.

Step 5: Keep it light. Inasmuch as possible, approach deliberate action as a way to shift the mood.

⇒ The more you think out scenarios by answering the questions, the easier it will be to come up with positive actions when you are in the "heat of the moment."

"Maintaining the parent-child connection requires attentiveness."

Chapter Five
Maintaining and Deepening
the Connection

"You will always be your child's favorite toy."
–Vicki Lansky

Maintaining and deepening the parent-child connection takes *discipline*. Unfortunately, for some the word "discipline" evokes negative memories or feelings of aversion associated with punishment, oppression, or abuse. Discipline, in my book, is not about being called to the front of the class to recite twenty "Hail Marys" or being subjected to corporal punishment. In other words, discipline is not about promoting mindless obedience, personal rigidity, or perfectionist attitudes.

My friend Linda is a mother of two boys ages ten and thirteen. She works full time as a teacher with "high-need" students. As a mom, wife, and teacher, she puts out a lot of

Consistent mindful parenting is comparable to becoming your own personal trainer.

energy each day toward meeting the needs of others. Over the years she has developed practices of self-discipline that make it possible for her to sustain a happy and healthy life.

In order to confront the demands of a busy work and family life, Linda set her intention to staying organized, focused, and on schedule. Among other things, she recognized a need for regular "alone time." As a result, she redesigned her daily schedule so that she could awaken rested at 5 A.M. She now has an early-morning "quiet time" just for her; the house is still, and she can cozy up, uninterrupted, on her couch with her morning coffee and newspaper. Linda says that this disciplined practice has, over a period of years, helped her be a better mom, wife, and teacher. Her pragmatic approach has allowed her to balance structure and stability with creative and open spontaneity. Her daily discipline has helped her sustain a relaxed, energetic, and content approach to life. Bravo, Linda!

When it comes to raising joyful and resilient children, discipline implies that we, like Linda, are taking a serious but balanced approach to the important work involved. It requires that we see and apply discipline in positive and constructive ways. Consistent mindful parenting is comparable to becoming your own personal trainer. Such self-training will engage you in regular mindful parenting practice and will influence you to seek out the support you need to fulfill your commitment to grow happier, healthier children.

Appropriate discipline:
- helps us refine desired behaviors, attitudes, talents, and skills
- supports healthy mental, emotional, and physical growth and development

- holds us to our commitments to accomplish what we have set out to do
- disrupts, through the use of intentional repetition, the habitual ways we live against ourselves and others
- enables us to overlay and eventually replace old counterproductive patterns of thought, emotion, and behavior with new learning suited to healthier, happier living

Maintaining and deepening the parent-child connection will work because you will make it work. In time, with regular practice, you will settle into your own unique style of disciplined mindful parenting.

Maintaining the Connection

Think of all the things in your life that require maintenance: car, checking account, personal grooming, home, and clothing. These are just a few obvious items that require some level of diligence. Maintaining the parent-child connection requires attentiveness also. Much like maintaining your car or your teeth, your commitment to these tasks prevents disasters down the road.

Maintenance means being protective and proactive as a parent. Proactive in the sense that the healthy connection you develop with your children is essential for them during their normal early development and during the times they need you the most. Your children's ability to rely on you as their "safe place and solid ground" will allow them to venture out on their own and come back when they need your

Maintaining the parent-child connection requires attentiveness also. Much like maintaining your car or your teeth, your commitment to these tasks prevents disasters down the road.

support. This is true at any age, whether your toddler is taking his first steps away from you or your teen is filling out her first job application. You will be the one they look for as they glance over their shoulders in search of assurance—*your* assurance. Why wouldn't they? You have always been the one they have counted on; why wouldn't you be there for the next new life challenge? Maintaining the parent-child connection requires ongoing attention, just like anything else that you want to keep in good condition. Here is an easy maintenance guideline you can follow to help you keep the connection you have with your child running on all cylinders.

Rehearsal

Reliability

Resilience

Renewal

Repair

Let me introduce you to some easy ways to maintain and deepen the parent-child connection, including the *Five Mighty R's* of daily maintenance, and the *Five Gems of Communication*.

The Five Mighty R's

Remembering and practicing the *Five Mighty R's* will help you maintain a stronger and healthier relationship with your children. They are *rehearsal, reliability, resilience, renewal,* and *repair*.

Rehearsal
Have you ever played an instrument in a band or had a part in a school play? If so, then most likely you learned that *if you don't make it to rehearsal, you will not be prepared to perform well*.

Whenever I am working with a client who wants to address a particular problem that involves interactions with others, I help them rehearse beforehand what they are going to say and do. Whether their goal is to settle a disagreement with a neighbor, ask for a raise, or set limits with their children, I want them to have appropriate and effective responses to whatever might happen during the interactions. As parents, the more we learn to anticipate our children's actions and responses, the more effective we are likely to be in gaining our children's understanding and cooperation.

What might such a mindful parenting rehearsal look like? Consider this example: Imagine a scene in which you, the mother, are speaking to your fifteen-year-old son:

Mom: "Jessie, I want you to be home at 9 P.M. If you are going to be even five minutes late, you need to call me. Are we clear on this?

Possible Response A: *"Oh Mom, don't be such a worrywart. I'll be fine."*

Mom: "You need to call me if you're going to be five minutes late. This is how you can continue earning my trust. Will you agree to do this?"

Possible Response B: *"But last week you said I could be home at 10 P.M. What's up with that?*

Mom: "What's up is that last week you came home fifteen minutes late, and I told you I would be pulling back your curfew time because you did not come home on time. This week I want you home by 9 P.M. Got it?"

Possible Response C: *"But Dad said he thought you were being too strict. I will go ask him when I need to be home."*

As parents, the more we learn to anticipate our children's actions and responses, the more effective we are likely to be in gaining our children's understanding and cooperation.

Rehearsals prepare

us to handle

surprises more

effectively; feel more

in control; and be

more concise and

to the point when

challenged by a

child's viewpoint or

by his expressions

of strong emotion

or defensive,

rude, blaming,

or minimizing

communication.

Mom: "Jessie, right now this is between you and me. I want to trust you and give you more leeway, but first you need to show me you are responsible enough to keep track of time and keep your agreements with me."

Invariably, parents quickly learn the value of taking time to rehearse what they want to say to their children. Rehearsals prepare us to handle surprises more effectively; feel more in control; and be more concise and to the point when challenged by a child's viewpoint or by his expressions of strong emotion or defensive, rude, blaming, or minimizing communication.

You can rehearse by repeating the practices prescribed in this book and then tailoring them to new situations. The more you apply these exercises to your parenting, the more natural mindful parenting will become. For example, when confronted with a challenge, mentally rehearse the three phases in the *Mindful Parent Happy Child* model—*Awareness*, *Self-Intervention*, and *Deliberate Action*—in relation to your specific challenge. Just as an athlete does, mentally rehearse ahead of time how you will move through the situation and attend to each phase. Envision yourself going through TINGLE in the self-intervention phase. Identify and choose to do something different in the deliberate action phase. Such practice takes energy and effort, but the payoff can be a new level of attunement, resonance, and trusting interaction between you and your child.

Resilience
Resiliency is an essential life skill. Observing how a person copes with and moves through stressful events is one of

the best ways to assess resiliency. When stressors occur—whether serious and life threatening or as simple as negotiating a change of address—how do you adapt? Are you able to keep a realistic and relatively relaxed perspective? Do you remain sufficiently flexible, or do you become overly rigid? Do you effectively work to stabilize yourself and the situations in which you find yourself, or do you devolve into more chaos and confusion?

In the field of humanistic psychology, resilience refers to an "individual's capacity to thrive and fulfill one's potential despite or perhaps even because of the stresses to which they are subjected" (Neill & Dias, 2006).

Consider the following characteristics of a resilient person as adapted from the work of health care consultant Dan Johnson (2010). As you go down the list, put a check next to the characteristics that you identify in yourself. Then take a moment to reflect on events in your life where you demonstrated resiliency.

Resilient people:

- have an ability to "bounce back" and recover from almost anything
- don't take "no" too seriously and are more apt to think, "Where there's a will, there's a way"
- view problems as opportunities to grow and develop, have fortitude during difficulties, make the most of a situation, even when they are disappointed
- often have a value system that drives them to seek deeper meaning
- claim a network of social support that helps them manage a variety of situations
- possess common sense and competencies for handling a wide variety of situations

Resiliency is

an essential

life skill.

- are comfortable and flexible in a wide variety of circumstances
- are realistic and accepting when faced with traumatic and life-changing events

Overall, resilient people have a capacity for self-renewal and restoration. Those who are less resilient are more likely to feel beaten down, helpless, and victimized when faced with negative stressors.

If you have come this far in the book, then you understand you have a significant challenge ahead. Mindful parents must develop resilience. If, as a parent, you often feel as though you are sliding two steps back with every step forward, seek out sources of encouragement and support. The remedy may be as simple as finding and contemplating sections or quotations in this book that you find uplifting and instructive. Or perhaps you need to reach out to a friend, therapist, or other mindful parents in your community. You might even create your own Mindful Parenting study and support group.

We are not all taught resiliency or had it modeled for us. Our own parents may well have fallen short in this area. Whatever the legacy you inherited from your family of origin, learning what resiliency looks like can be the first step toward learning how to develop it. When you have difficulty maintaining resilience on your own, do what it takes to help you stay focused on the positives. Here are some reasons why the practice of mindful parenting can require real grit:

1. Cultivating mindfulness—whether in the context of parenting or not—necessarily requires you to slip, make mistakes, and confront the obstacles that

Overall, resilient people have a capacity for self-renewal and restoration. Those who are less resilient are more likely to feel beaten down, helpless, and victimized when faced with negative stressors.

stand in the way of healthier, happier relationships.

2. At first mindful parenting will likely feel awkward and unnatural, which can arouse self-doubt and frustration. A sense of flow often comes slowly and is the result of repeated practice.

3. Results may not be as immediate as they seem to be in parenting programs that are more concerned with strategic interactions or behavior modification of children.

4. Mindfulness work can lead you to some very emotional and, at times, uncomfortable places. Honest self-appraisal is not always easy.

5. Mindfully taking full responsibility for yourself and your reactions can shake up your sense of self. Your ego will get toasted!

Such realities are why mindful parents need to develop resiliency and sources of encouragement and support. Without them, the work can be too mentally and emotionally frustrating.

Here are a few things you can do to develop resiliency as a mindful parent:

1. Choose to have an optimistic outlook in every area of life.

2. Take time for mindful moments throughout your day—during a few minutes of meditation, a walk around your neighborhood, or a nice meal or snack.

3. Manage your stress by setting boundaries and structuring your time to include good self-care. Learn how to say "no" if something is or may become a problem for you.

4. Learn to live from a place of acceptance. Life is an

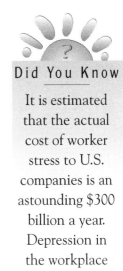

Did You Know

It is estimated that the actual cost of worker stress to U.S. companies is an astounding $300 billion a year. Depression in the workplace is costing U.S. companies an annual $44 billion a year.

ocean with many tides.

5. Focus primarily on what you have accomplished, not on what you haven't finished.

Reliability

Adolescent children reveal the level of their maturity as they demonstrate two distinct but interrelated attributes: self-reliance and responsibility. They gain our trust each time they call when they are going to be late, when they turn their homework in on time, when they take care of their hygiene, as they follow though on their commitments, as they make good decisions, and when they learn from their mistakes. Here's the challenge to parents and other caregivers: *What a child learns about reliability has a great deal to do with how reliable you are.*

As you demonstrate reliability in your interactions with children throughout their early years and beyond, they learn what they can and cannot count on from you. They also note if and how others can depend on you. Being reliable teaches your children they can trust you, and this becomes a significant gauge for them in other relationships—with friends, teachers, bosses, and life companions. If a child learns she cannot rely on her parent, she is more likely to have difficulty trusting others and/or have expectations that are too low. This can make her more prone to being taken advantage of. Being reliable sets a solid foundation for secure attachment in your child.

What a child learns about reliability has a great deal to do with how reliable you are.

EXERCISE

Parents instill and teach reliability by their actions. I have found it helpful for parents to step back and evaluate their reliability using the following statements. Each statement represents a nurturing or caretaking behavior. Use a 1-4 scale to list how often you engage in each behavior, with 1 = always, 2 = mostly, 3 = sometimes, 4 = never.

1. I pick up my children on time.
2. I serve nutritious meals.
3. I cooperate and coordinate with my children's teachers.
4. I listen carefully.
5. I tell my children I love them.
6. I check my children's homework.
7. I keep to a scheduled bedtime.
8. I ask about my children's day.
9. I talk with my children while driving in the car.
10. I know when my child is hungry.
11. I feed my children on a regular schedule.
12. I keep my children's bedding and clothing clean.
13. I keep track of who my children's friends are.
14. I get to know the parents of my children's friends.
15. I play games with my children.
16. I attend my children's events.
17. I encourage my children to try new things.
18. I make sure my children get a good balance of exercise and rest.
19. I have my children help me even if they don't do a good job or it takes more time.
20. I pay attention and respond with care to my children's moods.
21. I affirm my children for the things they do at least three times more than I criticize or punish them.

Now, go over your list. Highlight any item that received a 3 or higher. Note if any patterns emerge. For example, if you don't like cleaning house or you have a hard time managing time, higher scores in these areas may indicate areas of parenting that could use more attention and self-discipline.

For the areas in which you scored 1 or 2, affirm yourself. For those in which you scored 3 or 4, ask yourself the following questions:

- Is there anything I can change to be more reliable in this area?
- Do I need to ask for help?
- Are there any signs that my lack in this area is holding back or hurting my children?
- Do my children trust that I am going to take care of them in this area?

Notes: _____

_____

_____

_____

_____

This exercise can help you identify and prioritize areas of parenting and family life that could use mindful attention. Remember to stay away from judgment as you complete exercises such as this one. Mindfulness encourages one to observe and disrupt judgment of self or other, but in the end, it does not indulge it.

Now, take a few moments to assess what you want your children to rely on you for. Check any of the following numbered statements that represent what you would like them to experience in their relationship with you. Feel free to create additional statements. As you review the list, place one or more check marks by each statement to indicate the degree of importance to you. One check means "Important," two checks means "Very important," three checks means "Top priority."

I want my children to know and feel that:
1. They can count on three meals a day.
2. They are safe in our home and neighborhood.
3. Their school performance is important.
4. I will pick them up on time.
5. I am open to hearing their problems, joys, and worries.
6. I enjoy exploring life with them.
7. I am fair.
8. Their friends are welcome in our home.
9. Everyone has some need for personal time.
10. I will take responsibility for my mistakes.
11. I will communicate respectfully.
12. They can feel safe in sharing their emotions and experiences with me.
13. I am interested in their lives and activities.
14. I will do everything I can to keep them well and healthy.
15. They are individuals who matter.
16. They can have likes and dislikes that are very different from mine.
17. I will protect them from bullies and other potential sources of harm.
18. I will apologize when I have wronged someone.
19. I am forgiving.
20. I enjoy being their parent.

What would you like to add to the list?

21.

22.

23.

24.

25.

Now, reflect upon the following questions:
- What does being a reliable parent mean to me?
- What do I want my children to learn about being reliable people?
- Has this section on *reliability* changed anything? If so, how?

I have often told my family and friends, "You can trust that I will think about my part in a conflict or problem and take responsibility for it." This commitment to myself and others is a good thing to strive for, but the complex realities of life make it impossible to be perfectly reliable. In retrospect, there have been times when I have taken less responsibility for my part in a conflict or problem than I should have. (After all, I, like everyone else, have my own blind spots!) Nevertheless, I can see that most people know and feel they can rely on me because I am always aiming for full honesty and transparency.

As parents, we can only do our best. We will fail at being reliable and, at times, fail completely. But even these occasions can be turned into valuable learning opportunities for our children. There is nothing wrong with saying to your child, "I know I was late and kept you waiting. I am really going to work on this so you can have a better reason to trust me." Think of what it would have been like

As parents, we can only do our best. We will fail at being reliable and, at times, fail completely. But even these occasions can be turned into valuable learning opportunities for our children.

for you as a child if you had heard something like this from the significant adults in your life. Chances are, you would have trusted them more. At the very least, you would have been more likely to give them additional chances to prove themselves reliable.

Renewal

Take steps to renew yourself regularly:

- *Renew daily your commitment to be a mindful parent.* Refresh your vocation as a parent, mentor, or teacher with a bow, prayer, or some other sort of ritual. As you do this, don't be surprised if you feel maternal and paternal stirrings, perhaps, as a sense of purpose, love, and nurturing. Renewal of intention can arouse instinctive responses that are powerful enough to keep even the most exhausted parent going. How else can you explain functioning under conditions of sleep deprivation because your children need your attention in the middle of the night?

- *Plan time to recharge your batteries.* Brief breaks, catnaps, early morning quiet time, adult interaction, walks in nature, short retreats, vacations, and regular vigorous exercise are some of the important ways you can keep the parent-child connection vital and loving.

- *Tend with care the relationships you have with other adults who share life with you and your children.* The connections you have with spouses, partners, extended family, teachers, coaches, members of your spiritual community, and others with whom you have regular social interaction are part of an in-

Renewal is

essential. We

all need it, but

many of us have

developed a

bad habit of

shortchanging

ourselves to

the point that

we wind up

exhausted, angry,

or depressed.

terconnected web of support that helps keep your children safe and growing in the right directions.

- *Regularly turn your attention to thoughts of lovingkindness and plans to perform caring actions toward yourself and others.* When you first awaken in the morning, before you arise, give yourself thirty seconds to set your intention to parent mindfully. In addition, it may be helpful to make specific plans, as did one of the parents in one of my classes who was having a particularly difficult time with her twelve-year-old son and his unruly morning moods.

"I woke up and told myself, 'I am not going to react to my son's mood if he is grumpy this morning.' I lay in bed imagining ways I could keep myself from getting pulled into Foster's negativity. Once I had what I would do in mind, I set my intention: I am going to turn on some music if he is grumpy because I know he likes music; I am going to say 'good morning' to him and then leave him alone to work through his mood. I did just that. He did wake up grumpy, but neither one of us left the house mad or in bad moods. He even hugged me goodbye in front of his friends!"

Renewal is essential. We all need it, but many of us have developed a bad habit of shortchanging ourselves to the point that we wind up exhausted, angry, or depressed. I have found that mindful parents often renew themselves by talking and sharing with other parents. The laughter and the stories shared among parents in my mindful parenting classes bring fresh perspective, restored initiative, and renewed feelings of hope. Perhaps you can begin thinking about this: "How can I, on a regular basis, best renew myself and my commitment to mindful parenting?"

Repair

Something happens, and a stressful situation, a bad mood, or a curt comment triggers painful reactions and counter-reactions. Strong emotions well up, flooding the relationship with corrosive expressions of anger, hurt, guilt, shame, or blame. The parent-child connection becomes frayed, unravels, or snaps. When such experiences are repeated and left unresolved, those involved in the relationship become more vulnerable to ongoing feelings of frustration, helplessness, or despair.

Healthy relationships weather and even grow from such occasions because the people involved are able to work together to instigate relationship *repair*. When people are able to initiate successful repairs to the relationship, experiences of disconnection can actually strengthen the emotional bond between them and bring them closer together than before. Successful repair can be achieved in ways familiar to most of us, including the following:

- offers of an olive branch or an apology
- the giving and receiving of forgiveness
- an acknowledgement and acceptance of differing viewpoints
- a conscious shared effort to make amends

As previously suggested, parenting mindfully includes taking full responsibility for one's part in a conflict or problem. "I am the parent, so I don't need to apologize" is an attitude that can often operate unconsciously in the relationship between adults and children and compromise, or

Mindful caregivers tend and mend relational disconnections as they occur.

even prevent, efforts at relationship repair. Mindful care-givers tend and mend relational disconnections as they oc-cur. They are open to seeing and addressing the problems in themselves, their children, and the relationship without making themselves or someone else *the* problem. They resist sweeping trouble under the carpet, minimizing the feelings and experiences of others, and assigning blame exclusively to one party in a conflict.

As parents and adult caregivers, it is our job to initiate and accomplish repair in our relationships with children. When adults engage in efforts to repair, we are teaching and modeling essential relationship skills to our children. From us they can learn important lessons, such as the fol-lowing:

As parents and adult caregivers, it is our job to initiate and accomplish repair in our relationships with children.

- Everyone has bad days
- Mistakes keep us humble and help us grow
- Good relationships require that we take responsibil-ity for our actions
- Parents and other adults are fallible and imperfect

Oftentimes adults doubt the appropriateness of taking responsibility for their mistakes or weaknesses in front of children. Some fear they will appear "too soft," lose their child's respect, or weaken their caregiver authority. Taking responsibility for your share in a problem or conflict need not interfere with setting limits and boundaries with regard to your child's behavior. There is no need to fear that you will become "too soft." While it certainly would not be ap-propriate in *every* instance for a parent to talk about per-sonal foibles or how he or she is challenged by certain situ-ations, relationship repair inevitably requires it. Moreover, it is important to realize that one of the best ways to help a child lose respect for you and other adults is to try to convince them to "do as I say, not as I do."

What do you do when the parent-child connection has a gaping gash? At times like this, it can be helpful to remember and apply the acronym **STONE**. Let it be your "repair manual." As you practice introducing the elements of STONE into your relationships with the children in your care, you will be paving the way for a more trusting relationship with them.

The acronym STONE stands for:

- **S**how up
- **T**iming
- **O**wn it
- **N**o **E**xcuses

*S*how up

Showing up means making yourself available to your child to initiate repair. In order for the healing process to begin, it is important that, before you show up, you have restored a modicum of mental and emotional balance in yourself. To do this may require you to do the following:

- Take a few minutes to meditate. Sit or walk very slowly in a quiet area; focus on your breath; calm down.
- Check in with yourself by attending to your 5 Windows of Awareness. Guide your attention to the thoughts going through your mind and the emotions and body sensations you are feeling. Recover a sense of your interconnectedness with life in general and your child in particular.
- Attend to the parts of yourself that are not in balance. If you are hungry, have a snack. If you are

What do you do when the parent-child connection has a gaping gash? **STONE** is your repair manual.

Coming back

to them to heal

the relationship

opens the door

to understanding

and forgiveness.

upset about something else, compartmentalize this problem by filing it in an imaginary filing cabinet for attention later.

If you feel stressed or overwhelmed, create a list on paper of the things on your mind, or talk them through with someone who can listen supportively. This will help you reduce the noisy ruminations that can accompany mental and emotional overload.

- Before you *show up*, assess if you are ready to attempt a repair in the relationship. Ask yourself these questions:
  - Can I be sincere?
  - Can I be sensitive?
  - Can I be open?
  - Can I be honest?
  - Can I remain PRESENT and nonreactive?

If you can answer "yes" to these questions, you will be as ready as possible to begin the process of reestablishing your connection with your child.

As noted previously, your relationship with your child is nature's way of helping your kids get through life successfully. Showing up teaches your children that your relationship with them is paramount, regardless of how much hurt or anger has been experienced within and between you. Coming back to them to heal the relationship opens the door to understanding and forgiveness. When you "show up" to repair the wound in the connection, you are demonstrating your love for them as individuals and your commitment to be available … no matter what. Your child will feel this from you and believe in you. Perhaps, most important, you will teach them how to repair relationships with the other important people in their lives.

Timing

Timing is critical. When you show up to make a repair, be sensitive to how ready your child is to talk with you about the circumstances related to the points of disconnection in your relationship. Is your child mentally and emotionally ready to share in the work of repair, or can he or she be helped to become ready?

If you attempt a repair too early—if you are not emotionally ready or your child is not emotionally ready—then the repair is unlikely to hold. Remember, when we are flooded with strong feelings, we are usually not in a balanced place, and this can prevent us from processing information and communicating effectively.

Your child's age should influence how you approach the issue of timing. Toddlers and young children are at a stage of mental and emotional development that makes immediate efforts at repair more important. Keep your communication simple; for example: "Honey, I'm sorry I yelled at you. I shouldn't have. I will try not to do that again." Hug and interact with your child until you sense a reestablishment of attunement.

A teen may need time and space to themselves in order to cool down. If they reacted with hurt, anger, or some other negative emotion to something you did or said, they, like you, will benefit from having some time to process their emotions. You can approach your child with, "Hey, I feel like I need to talk about what happened between us. Is this a good time for you?" This shows respect for their process. If they say, "No. I am not ready," try to negotiate a future time

If you attempt a

repair too early—

if you are not

emotionally ready

or your child is

not emotionally

ready—then the

repair is unlikely

to hold.

for doing so. Among other things, this will show them that you respect them and their need to stabilize their thoughts and feelings before attempting to work things out with you.

Own it

Take responsibility for your part in a problem or conflict involving your child. If you lost control, own it. If you are the one having a tantrum, own it. We are all vulnerable to expressing reactions and behaviors that are not helpful or are hurtful to others and ourselves. Owning how we contributed to the rupture in a relationship takes courage and humility, but the benefits of doing so can be tremendous.

Here are a few examples of what "owning it" can look like:

If you were out of control and you yelled at your child, you might initiate repair with something like this: "*I yelled, and I know yelling is not helpful and can be hurtful and scary.*"

If you called your child a name: "*I am sorry I called you a name. This was wrong of me to do. I will do my best not to do this again.*"

If you were late: "*I am sorry for being late.*" (If your child asks why you were late, tell them the truth and be concise.) "*I was stuck in a line at the store*" or "*I ran out of gas*" or "*I got distracted and lost track of time.*"

Remember, you do not need to hide a mistake, if you made one. Whatever the truth is, your children will feel more connected to you if you are straight with them. When you "own it," you are teaching your children that it is safe

When you "own it," you are teaching your children that it is safe to make mistakes and important to be responsible for them.

to make mistakes and important to be responsible for them. Wouldn't it be nice if all adults—including teachers, CEOs, politicians, and other social leaders—behaved this way?

No Excuses

Once you have taken responsibility for your part in something, it may be tempting to justify or try to excuse your behavior. Excuses and attempts at self-justification come in a variety of forms. Using the above examples, here is what these different types of excuses can sound like:

Excuses and attempts at self-justification come in a variety of forms.

- Blaming: *"If you didn't make me so angry, I wouldn't have to yell."*
- Minimizing: *"You know I didn't really mean that you are lazy."*
- Rationalizing: *"If it were not for that slow woman in line, I would have been on time."*
- Intellectualizing: *"By the time the traffic cleared, I figured I was already going to be late, so I stopped at the store to pick up something for dinner."*

Making excuses for your mistakes will not help your children to trust you or help them feel secure in their relationship with you. Instead, they are likely to either hide their mistakes from you or develop perfectionist tendencies. Bite your tongue before making an excuse because if you don't, you are likely to nullify what you are trying to achieve.

Now that we have gone over the *Five Mighty R's* to maintain the parent-child connection, let's go over four specific ingredients that can help deepen the connection.

Really being

listened to and

heard by another

affirms that we are

not alone and that

we matter.

Listen First

Be Attentive

Be Expressive

Join

Deepening the Connection

Have you ever felt that you were the center of someone else's interests? Was it a parent? friend? life partner? pastor or rabbi? Can you recall what it was about their presence that made you feel like they were genuinely interested? Do you remember how you felt? Take a moment to reflect on this memory.

When someone takes time to communicate with us in a mutual and supportive way, we are likely to feel more secure and trusting and, as a result, draw closer to this person. Really being listened to and heard by another affirms that we are not alone and that we matter. It can strengthen the emotional bond we share with another. It can become so strong that we are moved to make vows of "till death do us part" in front of a room full of people.

People with caring friends and family members are fortunate to be at the center of someone's interest daily. Others get this experience by hiring a therapist to help them heal, live life more fully, and relate better to others. And still others have no one to hold them in heart and mind in an ongoing way.

Young children need to have a felt sense of being at the center of their parent's world. With older children, this need extends to, and is ultimately superseded by, relationships with their peers. These primary relationships either support or inhibit secure attachment, thereby influencing how we adapt and grow in life.

The Four Gems of Communication

The *Four Gems of Communication* can assist you in helping your children know and feel that they are consistently at the center of your attention. The *Four Gems of Communication* are: *listen first, be attentive, be expressive, and join.*

Listen First

Let your child talk first. While you are listening, consciously cultivate empathy by asking yourself, *"What is my child's point of view?"* More likely than not, it is very different from your own. If you and your child have a conflict, ask them what they feel the problem is or how they see the situation. Gently coax them to open up; invite them to talk about the disconnection in the relationship. Be direct in asking them what they are experiencing: "Do you feel upset with me because of something I've done?" or "I am wondering if you are hurting inside?" By taking the lead in discussing a delicate and emotional issue, you are sending a number of important messages, namely:

> *"In our family we talk about what is happening within and between us."*

> *"We care for one another and are not judgmental about how others feel."*

> *"Together we work on problems to find solutions."*

Children, at whatever age, are not automatically able to communicate what they are experiencing internally. They learn to identify, articulate, and clarify their thoughts and feelings as their adult caregivers encourage and support them in doing so. Sometimes they can use creative or more

Listening first will help your child feel it is safe to explore his or her emotional world while providing you the opportunity to get to know and understand your child better.

concrete images to identify feelings, such as "I have butterflies in my stomach," a sensation which they later learn to associate with fear or anxiety. Listening first will help your child feel it is safe to explore his or her emotional world while providing you the opportunity to get to know and understand your child better.

Be Attentive

As your child shares something about his or her experience or perspective with you, confirm your understanding of what they are saying to you. Do not assume what their experience is like for them. Do not confuse your own interpretation of what they are telling you with what their experience means to them.

You can help infants and toddlers develop clear associations between different aspects of their mental, emotional, and physical experience by frequently noticing, mirroring back, and reporting what you are seeing and hearing them do. Use appropriate touch often to reinforce your feedback, and adjust your tone of voice to be congruent with the behavior they are displaying. You can do this whenever and wherever you are with your child. For example:

"You are smiling. You look happy." (Possible touches: guided handclapping or a gentle stroking of the head. Tone of voice: happy!)

"Oh, look what you found: a big wooden spoon and a pan! . . . You are making such a big sound with them." (Here you may want to stand back and allow your child to explore the experience he or she is creating on the floor of your kitchen.)

Alternatively, you could initiate further play, exploration, and the experience of sharing by guiding the child to take turns with you hitting the pan with the spoon. Your tone of voice can be encouraging or somewhat excited.

Communicating this way provides children with the basic sense that the experiences they are having are real, verifiable, and worthy of attention. It reinforces a feeling in them of being safe and heard in the moment. It cultivates the development of their neural pathways in the direction of secure attachment.

Beyond the toddler stage, you can begin to let children know what you are seeing them do or hearing them say. Then you can encourage them to tell you if what you are seeing or hearing is accurate to them. Initially, neither agree nor disagree with what they are saying—this can come later, if needed. Such communication might sound something like this:

"What I am hearing you say is … (repeat what you hear). Do I have it right?"

"When you do that, I believe you may be feeling angry. Is this what it's like for you?"

As you repeatedly demonstrate to your child that you are interested in and able to understand his or her experience, you will not only help your child develop a greater sense of security, you will also help yourself understand how your child interprets the world around him with greater accuracy.

Finally, remind yourself that in most situations, it does not matter if your child's point of view or remembrances are

You can help infants and toddlers develop clear associations between different aspects of their mental, emotional, and physical experience by frequently noticing, mirroring back, and reporting what you are seeing and hearing them do.

similar to or different from yours. Much of the time, when your child sees or plans things differently from the way you see them, it is something to celebrate! In the end you want the children in your care to feel, sense, and believe that you are able to accept and understand them and that cultivating such a feeling in relationships is something to be valued and pursued.

Be Expressive

Your own expressiveness can encourage your children to continue communicating with you, or it can shut them down. How you direct your eyes, manage your tone of voice and body posture, apply touch, and choose words tells your children whether or not you are an interested participant in their life experiences. Some people are not very expressive when they are listening or talking. If this is true about you, try to become more expressive with your face. Your children begin to learn how to read your facial expressions and movements long before they can understand your words. Use your expression to mirror what you want them to know about themselves and how you feel about them.

Join

Joining with a child in his or her interests, fantasies, fascinations, and explorations goes beyond reflective and mirroring communication. The process can take a few minutes or many hours. Joining might involve something as simple as playing a game that a child creates or helping name her latest creepy-crawly pet. You can join with children by accompanying them to Disney World or to a movie. You also can join with them by asking about details in their daily lives. You can ask them how their friends are doing or about

How you direct your eyes, manage your tone of voice and body posture, apply touch, and choose words tells your children whether or not you are an interested participant in their life experiences.

their experiences with teachers. Follow up on the stories your children tell.

Then, when your teen pulls away from your hugs and answers your questions with a single word, accept it! Such behavior is symptomatic of their struggle to become individuals—a process that often involves keeping you as far away as possible while still wanting and needing your support and care. You can bridge the disconnections in your relationship with teenagers by asking open-ended questions, such as, "What was it like for you when you scored that goal?" and "What do you think your friend Sally is feeling right now?" Ask away!

While joining, it is also important to let your children see and enjoy the more playful, irreverent, silly, and creative parts of you. This helps them understand that it is okay, at times, to have and express feelings and impulses that are normally ignored or suppressed. This can only add to the sense of connection they will have with you.

The Thirty-Second Connection

When you come home to your child, meet him or her at school, or are otherwise reunited after a time apart, remind yourself to spend just "thirty seconds" communicating. In many instances, it only takes thirty seconds to make your child's heart sing.

When your child meets you at the door eager to tell you about her new science project or something else important to her, all you may want to do is put your things down, slip out of your work clothes, and unwind from the day.

Don't let this opportunity slip away. Be aware, and dis-

Joining might involve something as simple as playing a game that a child creates or helping name her latest creepy-crawly pet.

rupt your impulses to pull away. Do something different. Take thirty seconds to practice The *Four Gems of Communication*. This may be the best thirty seconds you can invest in your child's healthy development.

Greet and acknowledge your children. If they are expressing themselves in a whirl of excitement and words, listen intently, ask a few questions with bright eyes, and then tell them you want to hear more about their day after you change clothes. They may appear not to accept this plan at first, but they will get used to it. They need to know that you have wants and needs and that routines and boundaries are often important as we move through our days.

Take time to mirror back to your children who and how you experience them to be; affirm how fun, interesting, creative, and intelligent they can be. By showing such interest, you help your children learn about the joy and comfort a caring relationship can bring. With every thirty seconds you give, you will cultivate health, resilience, and confidence in your children. You will also be preparing them for times when they will have to manage and resolve the inevitable problems and worries that life brings.

To become a mindful parent, practice using the *Four Gems* throughout your garden of relationships. Give them a try and watch what blooms.

With every thirty seconds you give, you will cultivate health, resilience, and confidence in your children.

From Discipline to Freedom

This chapter opened with a brief discussion about discipline. It closes with a brief discussion about freedom because *discipline is necessary in order to enjoy freedom.*

Let me give you an example of how this is true. My calendar is a discipline I must maintain. I update it throughout the day. I keep it on my laptop, so it accompanies me just about everywhere I go. Everything I get done is mapped out in a color-coded schedule on my computer. I see a full week in front of me with a twenty-four-hour day for each day of the week. I break the twenty-four hours into manageable periods of time that remind me where I am going next and what I will be doing at any given time: blue blocks indicate "personal time," green blocks indicate "exercise," pink blocks stand for "work," and orange—well, you get the picture. Within the colored blocks I have notes, tasks, lists, and anything else that might fit.

All of this may sound obsessive, but preparing my calendar gives me freedom. I free my mind from excessive worries about missing something in my day or about what comes next. When I cannot access my calendar because of some technical malfunction or because I have misplaced my computer, I experience immediate distress. My mind becomes jumbled with worry and excessive mental activity as I try to reconstruct the lost information. I have difficulty staying present with myself and others. Conversely, I love the freedom a clear and stress-free mind gives me.

Similarly, maintaining and deepening the parent-child connection represents a disciplined set of practices that can lead to a greater sense of personal freedom. Using The *Five Mighty R's* and The *Four Gems of Communication* will initially take some effort and, perhaps, feel unnatural. In order to remember to practice these skills, you may need to do something different, such as writing them down on Post-its and tagging them to your refrigerator or your bathroom mirror. You may need to repeat them in your head, put them on flash cards, or make a memo to yourself on

Remind yourself that your discipline to maintain and deepen the parent-child connection is a sound investment with a potentially high rate of return. It can pay you back with less worry and more confidence as a parent.

your cell phone. To continue the discipline, there will be times you will need to tend the parent-child connection when you're busy, hungry, or tired.

Remind yourself that your discipline to maintain and deepen the parent-child connection is a sound investment with a potentially high rate of return. It can pay you back with less worry and more confidence as a parent. You can feel more assured knowing your child has a greater chance at thriving in life because of the way *you chose to parent*. By attending to your children's needs with consistency, you are inculcating in them greater internal capacities for remaining mentally and emotionally balanced.

To reiterate, children with secure attachment have healthier coping skills, more satisfying relationships, and do better in life. The discipline it might take to maintain and deepen the connection between you and your children can make all the difference in the kind of adults they become. The future survival and health of our families and our societies depend on this.

Quick Glance: Chapter Five

⇒ Maintaining and deepening the parent-child connection takes *discipline*.

Appropriate discipline

- helps us refine desired behaviors, attitudes, talents, and skills
- supports healthy mental, emotional, and physical growth and development
- holds us to our commitments to accomplish what we have set out to do
- disrupts, through the use of intentional repetition, the habitual ways we live against ourselves and others
- enables us to overlay and eventually replace old counterproductive patterns of thought, emotion, and behavior with new learning suited to healthier, happier living

Maintaining the Connection

⇒ Maintaining the parent-child connection requires attentiveness also. Much like maintaining your car or your teeth, your commitment to these tasks prevents disasters down the road.

⇒ Maintenance means being protective and proactive as a parent, in the sense that the healthy connection you develop with your children is essential for them during their normal early development and during the times they need you the most. Your children's ability to rely on you as their "safe place and solid ground" will allow them to venture out on their own and come back when they need your support.

The *Five Mighty R's*

⇒ Remembering and practicing the *Five Mighty R's* will help you maintain a stronger and healthier relationship with your children. They are *rehearsal, reliability, resilience, renewal,* and *repair.*

⇒ Invariably, parents quickly learn the value of taking time to rehearse what they want to say to their children. Rehearsals prepare us to handle surprises more effectively; feel more in control; and be more concise and to the point when challenged by a child's viewpoint or his expressions of strong emotion or defensive, rude, blaming, or minimizing communication.

⇒ Resiliency is an essential life skill. Observing how a person copes with and moves through stressful events is one of the best ways to assess resiliency. When stressors occur—whether serious and life threatening or as simple as negotiating a change of address—how do you adapt? Are you able to keep a realistic and relatively relaxed perspective? Do you remain sufficiently flexible, or do you become overly rigid? Do you effectively work to stabilize yourself and the situations in which you find yourself, or do you devolve into more chaos and confusion?

⇒ Adolescent children reveal the level of their maturity as they demonstrate two distinct but interrelated attributes: self-reliance and responsibility.

⇒ As you demonstrate reliability in your interactions with children throughout their early years and beyond, they learn what they can and cannot count on from you. They also note if and how others can depend on you. Being reliable teaches your children they can trust you, and this becomes a significant gauge for them in other relationships—with friends, teachers, bosses, and life companions.

⇒ Parenting requires a replenishment of our emotional, mental, and physical resources. We can restore ourselves by taking time for renewal.

⇒ Healthy relationships weather and even grow from such occasions because the people involved are able to work together to instigate relationship *repair*. When people are able to initiate successful repairs to the relationship, experiences of disconnection can actually strengthen the emotional bond between them and bring them closer together than before.

⇒ What do you do when the parent-child connection has a gaping gash? At times like this, it can be helpful to remember and apply the acronym STONE. Let it be your "repair manual." As you practice introducing the elements of STONE into your relationships with the children in your care, you will be paving the way for a more trusting relationship with them.

The acronym STONE stands for:

- Show up
- Timing
- Own it
- No Excuses

Deepening the Connection

⇒ When someone takes time to communicate with us in a mutual and supportive way, we are likely to feel more secure and trusting and then draw closer to this person. Really being listened to and heard by another affirms that we are not alone and that we matter.

⇒ Young children need to have a felt sense of being at the center of their parent's world. With older children, this need extends to, and is ultimately superseded by, relationships with their peers. These primary relationships either support or inhibit secure attachment, thereby influencing how we adapt and grow in life.

⇒ The *Four Gems of Communication* can assist you in helping your children know and feel that they are consistently at the center of your attention. The *Four Gems of Communication* are *listen first, be attentive, be expressive, and join.*

The Thirty-Second Connection

⇒ When you come home to your child, meet him or her at school, or are otherwise reunited after a time apart, remind yourself to spend just "thirty seconds" communicating. In many instances, it only takes thirty seconds to make your child's heart sing.

⇒ Take time to mirror back to your children who and how you experience them to be; affirm how fun, interesting, creative, and intelligent they can be. By showing such interest, you help your child learn about the joy and comfort a caring relationship can bring. With every thirty seconds you give, you will cultivate health, resilience, and confidence in your child.

"Practice acceptance and nonjudgment; there is no right or wrong way to being in the present."

Chapter Six
The Workbook: A Six Week Course for You!

"In the beginner's mind there are many possibilities.
In the expert's mind there are few."
–Shunryu Suzuki

By becoming familiar with the theories in this book and applying a few of its basic methods, you have taken specific steps toward becoming a more mindful parent.

This chapter offers a six-week course that will guide you into a more comprehensive practice of mindful parenting. It has been designed to help you do a little bit of work each day.

Allow me to offer some recommendations distilled from *Mindful Parent Happy Child* workshops and consultations I have facilitated over the years. To help you get the most out of these six classes, consider the following:

- Set aside fifteen to thirty-five minutes of uninter-rupted time daily. For six weeks make the course-work your number one priority, and put it on your calendar of activities. This will help you set and maintain your intention as you work at improving your mindful parenting skills.
- Carve out six successive weeks to give mindful par-enting the required daily attention. If you have a vacation coming up or other foreseeable interrup-tions, it may be better to delay the course until you have uninterrupted time to do so.
- Learn and frequently remind yourself of the five key practices for cultivating mindfulness. They are:
  - ➤ self-awareness
  - ➤ observation and reflection
  - ➤ description or identification of what is happen-ing in the present moment
  - ➤ a nonreactive acceptance of your internal expe-rience
  - ➤ an open, positive, and nonjudgmental approach to yourself and others

Now, let's begin!

Week 1: Beginner's Awareness Training

Objectives:
1. to develop awareness of the self as an integrated whole
2. to cultivate everyday mindful awareness practices

Start by Cultivating a "Beginner's Mind"
In this six-week class we will give you everyday practices to cultivate self-awareness. Cultivating *Beginner's Mind* is common in meditation practices. It means observing things as they are in the present moment, unburdened by assumptions, judgments, and interpretations. Each moment is an opportunity to practice having the mind of a beginner.

With *Beginner's Mind* pay attention to the Five Windows of Awareness: your five senses, along with the experiences of body, emotions, thoughts, and interconnectedness. (For a review of the Five Windows of Awareness, see pages 79-112.)

Through mindful awareness, parents can intentionally develop and more effectively maintain the all-important parent-child connection.

Exercises for Week 1, Days 1-6:
Meditation on the Five Windows of Awareness
TIME ALLOCATION: 15 MINUTES A DAY

Note: It is helpful to read this through a few times before doing it, or to have someone read and guide you through this exercise.

First Step:
Sit comfortably and close your eyes. Observe and follow your breath, inhaling and exhaling. If you observe your attention drifting away from your breathing, redirect it back to your breath. Continue to follow the cycle of your in-breath and out-breath. Allow yourself to stay immediately aware of what your breath does naturally. Attending to your breath oftentimes can stimulate a change in the rhythm of your breath-

ing. This is normal. Watch the rhythm. Familiarize yourself with it. Let it be. As Jack Kornfield says gently as he guides his meditations, "Let your breath breathe itself."

Do this for two to three minutes or more; become more comfortable with paying attention to your breathing. If you find it necessary to frequently redirect your attention to your breath—and you probably will—observe these internal movements toward attention to your breath as if you were at a distance. Practice acceptance and nonjudgment; there is no right or wrong way to be in the present. If you find your breathing shallow and rapid, deepen and slow it a bit to help you move into a more relaxed and focused state of mind.

Second Step:

With your breathing relaxed and regular, gently shift your attention to your five senses: sight, sound, smell, taste, and touch. Allow your awareness to move from one sense to another. Hold your attention on a particular sense for a minute or so before moving on to the next. When you're ready to transition from one sense to another, first bring your attention back to your breath. If your mind wanders, simply name what you see your mind doing—for example, "wandering," "thinking," "distracted," "worried"—then gently bring your mind back to your breath or to the sense upon which you were focused.

Here's what this might look like:

- *Sight:* With your eyes open or closed put your attention on what you see. If your eyes are open, look at one object or allow your gaze to float freely around you. Even when your eyes are closed, be aware of what is happening in the immediate, present moment. *See deeply in the present moment.*
  Breath . . . inhale . . . exhale . . .

- *Sound:* Become aware of the sounds around you. Listen to sounds that are close, and then shift your attention to more distant sounds. There may be familiar sounds that you are usually unaware of, such as the sound of your watch ticking. Pay attention to the details. *Listen deeply in the present moment.*
  Breath . . . inhale . . . exhale . . .

- *Smell:* Move your attention to your sense of smell. There is always something to smell. Whether you smell something cooking on the stove, the scent of flowers, or the exhaust from a passing vehicle, observe and note it. *Smell deeply in the present moment.*

    Breath . . . inhale . . . exhale . . .

- *Taste:* Gently shift your awareness to the sensations of taste. Notice what the inside of your mouth tastes like. Pay attention to the taste, even if you don't like it. Notice any subtle flavors you may not have been aware of before. *Taste deeply in the present moment.*

    Breath . . . inhale . . . exhale . . .

- *Touch:* Now attend to the sensations of touch. If your hands are on your lap, notice how the area feels where your hands and lap meet. Move your hands and notice what they are touching—whether it is an object, clothing, or skin. Spend some time being conscious of your experience. *Touch deeply in the present moment.*

    Breath . . . inhale . . . exhale . . .

Third Step:

Now, do the same with the other four Windows of Awareness.

- As you continue to focus on your breath, move your attention to the sensations and movements of your body. Starting from the top of your head or the bottom of your feet, allow your breath to continue cycling comfortably while you scan your body. Gently say "hello" to your body. Here you also can use the "Hellooo Body!" exercise you learned in chapter 4 on pages 88-89. If you find you are uncomfortable, acknowledge the area of discomfort and adjust yourself. If you are holding tension, use your breath to relax this area of your body by deepening your breath and exhaling fully. Continue this process until you are ready to move on.

- As you continue transitioning with your breath, allow yourself to become aware of your emotions. Identify—without identifying with—what you are feeling. For example, if you notice anger, observe it. If your mind wanders or avoids a negative emotion like sadness or regret, gently bring it back to attention and follow your breath. Notice the emotion's level of intensity and how it changes as time passes. Notice if your breath changes with the emotion. Sometimes an emotion will come and go like a wave. Do the same with other emotions you become aware of. If you begin to analyze an emotion or it pulls you into thinking about or remembering something specific, note this and return your attention to observing the emotion itself. Continue this process until you are ready to move on.

- Gently return to your breath; then move your attention to your thoughts. Observe that your thoughts are merely thoughts; they come and go like passengers on a subway. If you begin to get lost in a maze or storyline of thoughts, notice this without judgment. Simply note this as "wandering mind" and bring yourself back to observing your thoughts. Notice any changes in your breath as you watch your thoughts. Stay with this for a while as you allow thoughts to freely enter your mind without attaching to them. Continue this process until you are ready to move on.

- Return to your breath, and then expand your awareness to take in the complex interconnections that are a part of your being and experience. Notice the connections between the energy that is in and of you and the energy that surrounds you. Observe and reflect upon this network of interconnectedness by putting your attention on your heart. Keep your attention on your heart and begin to notice the energy of your intuition. What are you aware of? Who do you feel connected to? What do you enjoy doing the most? Reflect on these questions without thinking, but instead, with listening to a deeper part of you, a part you may call your *inner knowing*. Continue this process until you are ready to move on.

When you are ready, gently take a few deep breaths and open your eyes. Sit still for a moment before heading into your day.

Is this a challenge?

At times this exercise may seem boring or pointless. Initially it may also seem deceptively simple and unremarkable. When you try it for any length of time, you will find it quite challenging because you are actively disrupting attentional and physiological processes that heretofore have been primarily habitual and automatic. Intentionally focusing your attention and practicing awareness in the manner prescribed here is a key exercise for rewiring your brain. You can readily expect some resistance to such changes.

When you use your mind to intentionally focus your attention on something—for example, on a feeling of *appreciation*—you are triggering the firing of synaptic networks and sequences that can ultimately lead to the development of new neural pathways. Thus, with time and practice, you can become a more appreciative, patient, regulated person, or build whatever other traits you wish. Those in the neurological sciences borrow the saying, "What fires together, wires together" (Hebb, 1949). But you also can think of this process through the wisdom of Buddhist monk and teacher Thich Nhat Hanh: "One wonderful seed is mindfulness . . . Use every opportunity to touch that seed and help it to manifest on the upper level of your consciousness" (1994).

Exercise for Week 1, Days 4-6: Reflective Writing
TIME ALLOCATION: 15 MINUTES A DAY

On day 4 add the following exercise to your practice of attending to the Five Windows of Awareness. Now that you have taken a few days to practice mindful awareness in relation to five important aspects of yourself and your experience, you are better prepared to incorporate it into your daily life and stay better attuned to and in touch with yourself throughout the day.

First Step:

Take a few minutes throughout the day to press the "pause button" on your life and observe yourself in the present moment. Wherever you are—in your garden, car, kitchen, office, child's bedroom, or my favorite, the shower—use *beginner's mind* to press the "pause button" and attend to all the different aspects that make up your experience in the moment: your senses, your body, your feelings, your thoughts, and the interconnections with yourself and all that seems other than you. Try your best to be as if for the first time, without interpretation or assumption. Use *beginner's mind* to be present with your body, your feelings, your thoughts, and the realities of your interconnectedness.

Second Step:

Sometime during the day take a few minutes to write and reflect about what you became aware of when you pressed the "pause button". Keep a journal of your observed experience in a separate notebook. An entry might look like this:

Date: May 15
"Today, I stayed present to . . ."

My senses:
"I watched a fly on my sink. I smelled the shampoo in my daughter's hair. I listened to the sound of my coffee pot. I tasted the creamy tartness of yogurt. I felt the changing pressures of the hard plastic scoop in my hand as I cleaned the kitty's litter box."

My body:
"I observed that my body felt energetic in the morning. When I checked in around 3 P.M., I observed that my neck was tight and I was thirsty."

My emotions:
"When I paused around noon, I became aware I was feeling sad from some bad news I had received the day before. I was also aware that I felt anxious about all I had to get done before driving the kids to their after-school events."

My thoughts:

"When I took a few moments, I observed my thoughts were scattered and I was not focused. I also noticed I had a lot of worry-type thoughts. As I log this, I am observing that my thoughts are becoming more positive and peaceful."

My interconnectedness:

"When I was getting my children ready for school, I paused to reflect on the thoughts and feelings I have toward them. I took a moment to connect with my heart and consciously send my children heartfelt intentions of love and safety."

Now take a moment to practice in reference to your own experiences during the day:

Date:

"Today, I stayed present to . . ."

My five senses:

My body:

My emotions:

My thoughts:

My interconnectedness:

Exercise for Week 1, Day 7:
Commitment to an Everyday Practice
TIME ALLOCATION: 20 MINUTES

Now that you have an understanding of what it means to practice being mindfully aware throughout your day, you are better equipped to establish what you want your daily practice to look like. Your practice will change as you change, but for now, begin with what you can commit to realistically.

Refer to your log to examine the times and places you paused to observe yourself and your life. Note any patterns of experience and response that seem significant to you, including when you tended to do your reflective writing. This may help you come up with a daily mindfulness practice that fits naturally into your rhythm and routine. Now, answer the following questions:

1. How many times a day do I pause to be mindfully aware?

2. What times of day am I likely to do this?

3. Where am I when I press the "pause button" the most?

4. What am I doing when I pause to observe?

5. What time of day was I inclined to journal and reflect?

6. Where is the best location for me to do reflective writing?

Use your answers to help you think about when, where, and how you can turn your attention to cultivating mindful awareness. If you are more able to check in with yourself when you are in your car or blow-drying your hair, then start by making such occasions your prime time for practice. Give your answers some thought and write a detailed plan. Make it a declaration, if you like, such as, "I will practice mindfulness daily, especially when …." Have fun with this. Make it enjoyable, and most importantly, make it work with you and your schedule.

My Daily Practice:
"I will . . . _____"

As you continue this course for the next several weeks, you will find yourself settling into this process. You can look forward to the time when your practice becomes as natural as breathing.

Week 2: Know Thyself

Objectives:
  1. to better understand *why* and *what* you do as a parent
  2. to identify, modify, or discard the family heirlooms that create disconnection with your child

A Personal Inventory: Taking Stock of Family Heirlooms
People who have taken the time to understand themselves and the history and network of their family relations seem to do better in life. In part that is because they have worked to understand how their patterns of thought, emotion, and behavior are rooted in their history and experience as they were growing up. Becoming a mindful parent involves a similar journey—coming to know you better. As you gain knowledge of who are you, you become aware of choosing to live similarly or differently in relation to people and dynamics that influenced your formation as a person. With such choices you gain the power and insight necessary to make changes in your ways

of relating to yourself and the world around you.

When we work to understand our families of origin and what they have and have not given to us, it is better to do so with an open mind and forgiving heart, and then take complete responsibility for our lives and how they unfold from this time forward. If we fail to do so, we will remain vulnerable to regarding ourselves more as victims who cannot change than as beings who have the ability to choose and work for meaningful change in ourselves and in the lives we live.

A corresponding attitude of acceptance is also important. In accepting the treasures and limitations we received from our families, we can gain a clearer sense of where we must start addressing and resolving any anger, hurt, shame, or guilt, along with other constraining habits of emotion and thought that can keep us from a path of personal growth. In the *Mindful Parent Happy Child* program, acceptance means we honestly and unapologetically acknowledge the principle players, significant events, and environmental contexts that have contributed to our formation as persons, and we seek to understand their current impact on who and what we are becoming.

☼
Exercise for Week 2, Day 1: Awareness of Family Patterns
TIME ALLOCATION: 30 MINUTES
Review: pages 45-49

This week is focused on exploring your family across generations. You began this process with the questions you were asked in chapter 2 page 45-49. Before going any further with this section, go back to that exercise and reflect upon your responses to those questions. Look at your answers carefully, and ask yourself if there is anything you would like to add or amend. Once you have done this, you are primed and prepared to take a deeper look at your family's patterns of thought, emotion, behavior, and reactivity.

First, lay out a family tree. It might be easiest to use columns, but do whatever works best for you. For each member of your family and extended family, come up with a list of words that best describes them. For example, you may write something like *"Uncle Larry: lighthearted, joker, and religious."* Include grandparents (on both sides), parents, siblings, aunts, uncles, first cousins, and others who played an important role in your childhood.

Next, note any prevailing circumstances that influenced how these family members interacted and functioned. This might include such patterns as the following:

Addiction: Note the types of addiction(s): *nicotine, prescription medications or street drugs, gambling, work, spending, pornography*

Mental Illness: Identify and locate those people and relationships affected by *depression, bipolar disorder, difficult personalities, symptoms related to trauma or chronic stress, schizophrenia, or other pervasive dysfunctions of thought, emotion, and behavior (e.g., extreme suspiciousness, explosive anger or rage, suicidal thoughts or attempts, or eating disorders).*

Physical Illness: Consider the impact of physical disease and processes of medical treatment in your family. Pay attention to things like *cancer, injuries from accidents, diabetes, heart disease, multiple sclerosis, chronic pain or fatigue, and other chronic health problems.*

Abuse: Note any patterns of *psychological, physical, and/or sexual abuse— or reactions to such abuse—and neglect* that emerge within a generation or seem to get passed on from one generation to the next.

In order to build a more comprehensive picture of your family, catalog your observations according to the following format or something similar.

Last, be certain to include a profile of yourself.

Italics represent fictional examples.

Name of Family Member: *Margaret*

Relation to Me: My *aunt, my father's sister*

Current Age (if living):

Deceased: *1998* Cause of death: *Lung cancer*

Adjectives that best describe this person:
Sensitive, caring, and lonely.

Incidences or patterns of addiction:
At holiday gatherings she drank a lot, and a few times I found her crying in the bathroom.

Mental and physical illness:
None. Maybe depression.

Abuse experienced or transmitted by this person to others:
My grandfather was verbally abusive toward her because he wanted a boy when she was born.

What was this person's religious or philosophical orientation?
Atheist.

What did the family expect of this person? What significant role(s) do or did he or she play in helping or hurting the family?
Everyone thought she was fun. She just drank too much and smoked like a chimney. She got mad when my mom wouldn't let her smoke in the house. One time she threw her glass of scotch at the wall.

What impact has this person had on you? What legacy do you see in yourself that has been passed on from or through him or her?
I didn't like it when she drank. I thought she was funny, but she also seemed sad. I didn't like the way she looked out of control. I don't drink except for a glass of wine on a rare occasion.

☼
Exercise for Week 2, Day 2: Studying My Family Tree
TIME ALLOCATION: 30 MINUTES

Now that you have a complete outline of your family, look more closely at the "heir-looms" you have inherited. Using your work from the previous day, note patterns of similarity and difference between you and other members of your primary relationship network.

First Step:
Place an asterisk next to each description that fits both you and one or more family members. For example, if you and four other family members have or have had cancer, mark each person so affected. Also note the types of cancer the others have had and whether or not a specific type is more prevalent than others. Do the same with any other patterns you notice.

Second Step:
Answer the following questions:

1. My parenting style tends to be (check those that apply)

    distant _____   understanding _____

    guilt ridden _____   loving_____

    angry _____   happy_____

    worried _____   encouraging_____

    overwhelmed_____   positive _____

    tired_____   strategic_____

    stressed _____   other _____

2. How did your mother show you that she loved you? _____

3. How did your father show you that he loved you? _____

4. List three words that best describe how others perceive your mother (friends, neighbors, and other).
   1)_____ 2)_____ 3)_____

5. List three words you would use to describe your mother.
   1)_____ 2)_____ 3)_____

6. List three words that best describe how others perceive your father (friends, neighbors, and other).
   1)_____ 2)_____ 3)_____

7. List three words you would use to describe your father.
   1)_____ 2)_____ 3)_____

8. List three words you would use that best describe you.
   1)_____ 2)_____ 3)_____

9. The family patterns I am most likely to pass down to my children are

   _____

   _____

10. When I consider my family patterns, I feel _____

11. What I have learned from doing this exercise is_____

    _____

When you have finished this exercise, sit quietly and observe what you experience in the present moment. If you are feeling uncomfortable, make note of "uncomfortable feelings." If you are judging, make note of "judgment." Sit still and notice your breath. Inhale and exhale for a few moments before you leave the place where you have been working.

Exercise for Week 2, Days 3-7: Changing Your Family's Legacy
TIME ALLOCATION: 30 MINUTES A DAY

First Step:
Begin this exercise with quiet meditation. As in the very first class, use your breath and your attention to the Five Windows of Awareness to settle into more immediate awareness of your whole self. Take as long as you need.

Second Step:
Look over your responses from yesterday. Be aware of any negative judgments or feelings toward yourself or others. Remind yourself that you are not blaming or being disloyal to your parents or other family members by exploring and analyzing. You are simply gaining information that will help you make better sense of your life and allow you to make healthy choices that will maintain and deepen the parent-child connection.

Reflection questions:
1. What insights have you gained about your family and yourself?

_____

_____

2. What I like most about how I was parented is

_____

_____

3. The generational family patterns I want to keep are

- _____

- _____

- _____

- _____

4. The generational patterns I want to change are

- _____

- _____

- _____

- _____

Third Step:

For the rest of this week as you awaken each morning, spend three minutes observing and becoming aware of your breathing. You can do this lying in or sitting on your bed or sitting at the kitchen table. Devote yourself to being mindful of the family patterns passed on to you. Begin to set your intention on certain patterns you want to change. If you want to stop yelling, begin to break the family pattern by setting your intention to stop yelling, and so on.

Week 3: Applying the MPHC Model

Class Objectives: to become more skilled in applying the MPHC model

Now that you are increasing your awareness and have a better understanding of your family's legacy to you, you can begin putting the *Mindful Parent Happy Child* model to specific use. In this class you will be given daily exercises that will help you incorporate the model into actual parenting situations. We will begin by reviewing the three different phases and components of the model found on pages 57-94.

Exercise for Week 3, Days 1-3: Mindful Awareness
TIME ALLOCATED: OCCASIONS YOU CHOOSE
THROUGHOUT EACH DAY PLUS 15 MINUTES
OF REVIEW AT THE END OF EACH DAY
Review: pages 76-126

First Step:

For three days keep a notebook and pen with you at all times. (This may be the most challenging part of the exercise!)

Second Step:

Throughout the day use specific parenting situations to practice present moment awareness with your children. Jot down notes: the thoughts and emotions you are aware of and the behaviors and reactions that accompany them. Your notes might look something like this:

"I am aware that I am hungry and not listening to my child talking to me."

"I am aware that I feel guilty for yelling at my children and that I am trying to make up for it by giving in to their demands for a later bedtime."

"I am aware that my back is aching and that I am complaining a lot. I am becoming increasingly short tempered with my children."

"I am hurt that my child is pushing away from me and that she doesn't seem to appreciate all that I am doing for her. I am reacting with disappointment and frustration, and I notice that I feel like pushing her away too."

Third Step:

At the end of the day take ten minutes in a quiet place where you can review your notes. Close your eyes and focus on each of the noted experiences. Consciously recall each situation, and imagine yourself responding in a way that will strengthen your connection with your child. Review the revised scene.

Using the first two scenarios from above, your re-imagining might look something like this:

"I am aware that I am hungry. I see myself listening to my child while I am fixing us a snack we can enjoy together. I see my child smile at this, and I see me smiling back."

"I am aware that I feel guilty for yelling at my children. I ask them to sit down with me for a moment. I apologize for yelling at them and acknowledge to them that there are better ways for me to handle my frustration. I invite them to examine with me different ways to manage feelings and emotions. I see myself working with my children to come up with creative ideas that we can all practice as a family. We are working together, and this feels good."

Exercise for Week 3, Days 4-5: Self-intervention
TIME ALLOCATED: 15 MINUTES AT THE END OF EACH DAY
Review: pages 126-134

In this section you will focus on phase 2 of the MPHC model. You will practice applying a self-intervention when you feel out of balance—in other words, whenever you are unable to regulate your emotions, thoughts, and behaviors in ways that positively support the relationship between you and your child. To bring yourself back into a self-regulated state, apply the easy-to-use TINGLE method.

First Step:
Keep your notebook handy and write down situations or circumstances (with children present or not) when you became overwhelmed or out of control.

Second Step:
At the end of the day review each incident and record a helpful alternative self-intervention you might have used. Use the following TINGLE outline. The outcome might look like this:

The incident:
   "I am aware that my back is aching and that I am complaining about everything. I am aware that I am becoming increasingly short tempered with my children."

A Sample Self-Intervention Using TINGLE:
   Timeout: "I make sure my children are taken care of, and then I tell them that I am going to take a few minutes to myself."

   Inhale-exhale: "I lie on my bed and close my eyes. I focus on my breathing, following the inhale and exhale of each breath. I slow my breathing and make it deeper to encourage relaxation and self-soothing."

Name It: "I ask myself what is going on with me. I know my back is hurting, and I realize I have done nothing to take care of it. My aching back is causing me to be reactive with my children. My children are just being kids."

Ground Yourself: "I remind myself that I am imperfect and that I am going to have bad days. I remember that mindful parenting is something I practice. I am practicing mindfulness as I lie on the bed for this timeout. I commit that I will rest my back and take better care of it from now on."

Loosen-up: "Even though my back hurts and I have been irritable, I can still stay lighthearted and keep my perspective. I remember that my children are forgiving when I am grumpy. I can even laugh at myself for how grumpy I can be."

Evaluate Your Mind: "Before I end my timeout, I check to make sure my mind is able to control my feelings, thoughts, and behaviors. I do this by asking myself the following questions":
- Am I able to think clearly?
- Has my level of emotional arousal decreased? *(Use a 1-5 scale.)*
- Is my body settled down and relaxed?
- Can I think creatively?
- Can I express words and actions that model love and leadership?
- Can I find a solution that teaches my child something about life?

Now think of a real-life encounter where you would like to apply the TINGLE method, and practice by filling in the following information.

My self-intervention could have been
Timeout

_____

_____

Inhale-exhale

_____

_____

Name It

_____

_____

Ground Myself

_____

_____

Loosen-Up

_____

_____

Evaluate Your Mind

- Am I able to think clearly? _____
- Has my level of emotional arousal decreased? _____
- Is my body settled down and relaxed? _____
- Can I think creatively? _____
- Can I express words and actions that model love and leadership? _____
- Can I find a solution that teaches my child something about life? _____

☼
Exercise for Week 3, Days 6 and 7: Deliberate Action
Time allocated: 15 minutes at the end of each day
Review: pages 134-140

At the end of the day revisit your quiet place and pull out your notebook. You can use the same examples to practice this exercise, or you can use more immediate ones. Remember, in the *Deliberate Action Phase* of the model you are devising a plan of action to promote the parent-child connection. If there has been a disconnection during a tense or emotionally charged situation, then this is the time to reconnect. After you have used the TINGLE method to guide you back into an emotionally regulated state, you will see how natural it is to think strategically and begin creating a plan to nurture the connection.

Recall situations during the day for which you would like to devise an intentional plan. Use the following format:

The situation:

_____

_____

The goal:

"What I want to achieve is _____

_____."

The strategy:

"I can be effective in helping my child follow my lead by _____

_____."

The desired outcome:

"I will help my child begin working with me by _____

_____ ."

Life skills to be taught:

"I will use this as an opportunity to teach life skills, such as _____

_____ ."

Keeping it light:

"I will keep our reconnecting time light and continue acting as a leader to my children

by _____

_____ ."

If you follow this format for the rest of this week and into next week, the three phases of the *Mindful Parent Happy Child Model* will begin to feel more natural, and you will begin to feel more confident as a mindful parent. Daily mindfulness in all you do will enable you to recognize and intervene when you are getting out of balance with your whole self and allow you to experience deeper joy in your parenting.

Week 4: Practicing Being a Mindful Parent

Objective:

1. to integrate the Three Principles of MPHC into action
2. to further the incorporation of mindfulness practice into daily life

Being a mindful parent is, ultimately, a way of being; it is not just a set of things you do. In this section, you will begin to develop your practice through brief periods of meditation and by integrating the Three Principles of mindful parenting into your daily routines. Intentional focus on mindfulness, combined with daily practice, develops a mindful brain.

⚙

Exercise for Week 1, Days 1-7: Sit and Be Still
TIME ALLOCATED: 10 MINUTES TWO TIMES A DAY

An invitation to meditate may trigger a sudden impulse to abandon this whole mindful parenting thing. After all, many of us are not comfortable with sitting still and being quiet. Besides, pausing to practice mindful awareness in the moment is not what most motivational speakers suggest. More likely they suggest that you get up and get moving, right? Unfortunately, people who tend to be motivated by charismatic energy from a speaker or leader often find that once their self-help "high" dissipates, they have trouble rediscovering energy or direction. Meditation helps train our minds to discover what is true for us. With meditation we can explore what motivates us, and we can ride the ever-changing tides of emotion and thought with greater acceptance and flow. These internal changes come through our own doing, and they require patience and persistence.

Practice sitting comfortably and quietly two times a day for ten minutes each time. Lock yourself in the bathroom if you have to. At least there, you always have a good seat! However, what is most important is not where or when you sit quietly, but that you do it consistently. The hardest part of meditation for me has been letting go of those things I feel I "should be doing" so that I can be still. If you really want to explore meditation practice, there are many resources available. I have a list of some on the www.mindfulparenthappychild.com Web site. For now, keep it simple. Schedule twenty minutes into your day. Work at being consistent in your practice because this is the surest way you can realize the benefits of meditation.

Here are some suggested steps you can follow:

- Find a comfortable place to sit. It can be in a chair, on a couch, on a cushion, or anywhere that will help you relax. I advise against lying down because this will relax your body too much, and you will fall sleep. Sleep is not meditation. It is sleep.

- Close your eyes and take one or two good, deep breaths. When you exhale, try to empty all the breath from your lungs and abdomen.
- Then put your focus on your breathing . . . inhale . . . and exhale, and repeat this for a few minutes.
- When your mind begins to wander, which it will, take note of this and say to yourself "wandering mind." Then bring your focus back to your breath . . . inhale . . . exhale.
- If you judge the process or yourself, such as "This is boring" or "I can't stand this" or "I am so bad at this," take note of this judgment and say to yourself "judging." Then bring your focus back to your breath . . . inhale . . . exhale.
- If your notice emotions coming up, do the same as you would for your thoughts. Tag them by noting "*sadness*" or "*fear*" or "*joy*" or whatever else you are experiencing. Then bring your focus back to your breath . . . inhale . . . exhale.
- Continue this process. When your mind wanders off, identify and name what is happening. Then focus on your breath as you return your attention to a state of free-floating awareness.

This is one approach to meditation that you can use in the course of your busy life. It seems so simple, yet—as most beginners soon realize—it often is not easy to sustain. Meditation requires patience, more patience, and then a little more patience.

Now let's turn to the Three Principles of Mindful Parenting and begin weaving them into everyday awareness.

Exercise for Week 4, Day 1: All Adults Are Parents
DAY 1
TIME ALLOCATION: 20 MINUTES ANYTIME
Review: pages 55-56

First Step:
Answer the following questions in your notebook:

1. Can I commit to seeking a loving and mutual connection with *all children*, even when they are not my own? Yes or No (circle)
    (If you answered *yes*, continue on to question 2. If you answered *no*, go to question 6.)

2. What are the ways in which you are a parent to children other than your own?

    _____

    _____

3. Why is this role important to you?

    _____

    _____

4. What situations are the hardest to act on as the parent of another person's child?

    _____

    _____

5. What are things you can do today to practice being a parent to all children?

    _____

    _____

6. What makes it difficult to accept the role of being a parent to all children?

    _____

    _____

7. In your role as a parent to all children, is there something that creates internal conflict? If so, explore this and describe it here?

_____

_____

8. If there is a principle you would like to replace this one with, what might it be?

_____

_____

Please understand that you are not required to accept and practice this principle in order to be a mindful parent. Rather, it is promoted as a basic principle designed to promote mindfulness and high-quality connections with as many adults and children as possible. The *Mindful Parent Happy Child* program accepts everyone as a valuable individual, and in an effort to live mindfully, we support a wide array of practices.

Exercise for Week 4, Day 2:
Parent Child Connectedness Grows Happy Children
Time Allocation: 20 minutes anytime
Review: pages 57-64

First Step:

Find a quiet place and take out your notebook. Reflect on each of the following questions before answering. In this context, the word "seed" means those values, qualities, and ways of being that can be intentionally planted into your child's world of experience, even as you continue to acknowledge and respect your child's uniqueness and value as an individual.

1. What seeds (compassion, integrity, love) do I want to sow and nurture in my children?

    _____

2. What seeds do I have available within me to pass down to my children?

    _____

3. What seeds do I want to nurture in me?

    _____

4. How do I want my children to see themselves?

    _____

5. How do I want my children to view the world?

    _____

Second Step:

This step will help you begin to identify those attitudes, judgments, and expectations that often interfere with deepening and maintaining the parent-child connection. By following the example below, reflect on and write down anything that is triggered in you by your child. This step can be difficult because usually we do not want to think of ourselves as annoyed by or judgmental of our children. Try to come up with as many scenarios as you can. The more insight you gain into these areas, the more you can make changes to cultivate your child's connection with you. In other words, if you don't like some of the seeds you are planting now, you can begin planting different seeds.

Here is a sample exercise:

Scenario:

"I don't like that my eight-year-old son is so sensitive. I can't give any correction without him crying. I want him to be strong so that he can stand up for himself."

Judgment: *"My son is too sensitive for an eight-year-old."*

Expectation: *"My son needs to be able to take care of himself."*

The negative seed

I am planting: *"My judgment and expectation may cause my child to feel ashamed of himself. The underlying message is, "You are not good enough.""*

Insight: *"Perhaps he cries when I correct him because he feels afraid of or hurt by my judgments."*

I can change: *"I can accept that my child is sensitive and help him develop this natural quality in a positive direction. People who are sensitive can be more empathic toward others. I can mirror empathy in my response to him, which will water the seed of empathy. I can be empathic as well as directive when I need to be, and I can help him learn to set internal boundaries so that he can be a sensitive and caring person who can also take care of himself in a variety of situations."*

Now it's your turn. Over the next few days come up with your own parenting situations by using the following outline as your guide:

1) Scenario:

    Judgment:

    Expectation:

    The negative seed
    I am planting:

    Insight:

I can change:

2) Scenario:

Judgment:

Expectation:

The negative seed
I am planting:

Insight:

I can change:

3) Scenario:

Judgment:

Expectation:

The negative seed
I am planting:

Insight:

I can change:

4) Scenario:

Judgment:

Expectation:

The negative seed
I am planting:

Insight:

I can change:

☀
Exercise for Week 4, Days 4-7: Mindful Parenting Is a Life Practice
Time allocation: 20 minutes anytime and throughout the day
Review: pages 64-70

So far you have been deepening your own capacities for mindful awareness and your applications for *being in awareness* in each moment of parental work. As we have seen, mindfulness practice in parenting requires being the Observer of our whole self—our senses, body, thoughts, feelings, and interconnectedness. In this section you are given exercises that will help you strengthen your skill as an Observer of you.

In chapter 1, page 14, I disclosed that when I catch myself doing something critical or unhelpful, I imagine my Observer making observations in a distinctive voice. This has helped me differentiate when I am observing from when I am not. You might try a similar tactic to see if this is helpful for you as well.

First Step: Practice Observing
10-minute Mindfulness meditation:
- Find a comfortable place to sit. It can be in a chair, on a couch, on a cushion, or anywhere else that will help you relax.
- Close your eyes and take one or two good, deep breaths. When you exhale, try to empty all the breath from your lungs and abdomen.
- When you are ready, focus on your breathing . . . inhale . . . and exhale.
- When you notice your mind beginning to wander, watch this mental activity from the standpoint of the Observer, and simply note to yourself "wandering mind." For a moment observe your wandering mind, but do not get pulled into or "lost" in it. Don't try to push it away. Observe from a more neutral standpoint, as if you are watching your thoughts from the top of the Empire Sate Building.

Now apply this process with the Five Windows of Awareness to your 1) five senses, 2) body, 3) thoughts, 4) emotions, and 5) sense of interconnectedness within you, with others, and with the larger world.

- I am the Observer of my five senses.
- I am the Observer of my thoughts.
- I am the Observer of my emotions.
- I am the Observer of my body.
- I am the Observer of my sense of being interconnected.

Using this approach, practice ten minutes of mindfulness meditation every day. Eventually, try to build this practice to fifteen or twenty minutes a day. Try two briefer periods of meditation or a single, longer meditation. When you find the practice of awareness difficult, remind yourself of the proven benefits of meditation: It calms negative responses to stress, strengthens the immune system, and enables the cultivation of clearer thinking and healthier social interaction.

Second Step: Being The Observer

When I sit, walk, or chat with a friend, or work with a client, the inner voice I use, described on page 14, helps me be the Observer of my inner life. As the Observer I can peer through the Five Windows of Awareness and be in the present moment. This allows me to be a better monitor of myself and sets the stage for more effective self-intervention. The following is an example:

When I observed myself being judgmental, I imagined the Observer's voice saying:

"Well, look at that, Pilar. You just put_____(name)_____ down for doing that thing you don't like. Now what are you going to do to help_____(name)_____ feel loved and connected to you?"

When I have observed myself being testy and irritable:

"You're tired and hungry, but try not to act like a big, ol' crab cake.
"Why don't you find time for a ten-minute catnap? This will help you feel better."

When I have observed myself having an emotional response to something:

"Wow! That's a big feeling bubbling up. Is this an appropriate and helpful response to the situation?

When I have observed myself disconnecting with someone because I feel hurt, angered, or something else by them:

"You know, Pilar, try looking at this through the lens of caring for others rather than from your own sense of pride and self-importance."

Your turn! Over the next four days, as you attend mindfully to the Five Windows of Awareness, cultivate the practice of being the Observer.

Develop an inner voice for your Observer. Create a voice that will talk to you in a nonjudgmental way but also will serve as a guide to help you stay in present-moment awareness.

When I observe feelings of _____, the Observer can say:

" _____ ."

When I observe thoughts of _____, the Observer can say:

" _____ ."

When I observe myself disconnecting with _____ because

_____ :

the Observer can say: " _____

_____ ."

When I observe my body feeling _____, the Observer can say:

"_____

_____."

When I observe my behaviors of _____, the Observer can say:

"_____

_____."

Week 5: Mindful Communication

Class Objectives:
1. to develop awareness of how I communicate with others
2. to integrate mindful communication skills for the continuous deepening and maintenance of the parent-child connection

As discussed on pages 147-173, maintenance of the parent-child connection is proactive in nature. It is supported by the intention to *be* a better parent. This week, during your meditation set your intention to practice *mindful communication*.

Attending to what and how we are communicating is a key mindfulness practice because we human beings are always communicating something, even though we often are not conscious of it. The fact is, if you don't take care for how and what you are communicating, you will be much more likely to communicate with your children and others in inconsistent, incongruent, and ineffective ways.

☀

Exercise for Week 5, Day 1: Evaluate Your Ways of Communicating
TIME ALLOCATION: 30 MINUTES TOTAL,
15 MINUTES OF MINDFULNESS MEDITATION AND
15 MINUTES OF REFLECTIVE WRITING

Our ways of communicating are largely an inheritance from our primary caretakers and adolescent peer community. Whether you had parents who communicated in a style that made you feel comforted, safe, and heard, or anxious, insignificant, and unworthy, you likely adopted an approach similar to theirs. How you communicate is inculcated or programmed through your interactions with others while you are growing up. Fortunately, a healthy brain is capable of new growth and adaptation, and with the right kind of practice, it is quite possible to alter how we give to and receive messages from others.

This first class will help you become aware of how you communicate today, and how your primary caretakers influenced your style of communication. Answering the following questions will help you identify areas of change you would like to make. Remember, you can change your brain's neural pathways by setting your intention and using awareness practices to address what you want to change.

Sometime during the day answer the following questions. Before answering the questions think about the following styles of communication and try to identify which category your parents or primary caretakers fit into. Identify which ones you fit into.

Situation: Giving a teenager the task of going to the store to pick up a few grocery items.

- Assertive   "I want you to go to the store before noon."
- Timid   "I was wondering if it would work out for you to go to the store around, say, noon?"
- Passive   "It would be helpful if you could go to the store around noon."
- Aggressive   "You need to get your lazy butt to the store by noon! Got it?"
- Passive/
  Aggressive   "You can go to the store when you want to, you never listen to me anyway."

- Indirectly: "Gosh, I really need those items from the store before noon."
- Guilt "I want you to go to the store, and for all I do for you, I want you to do it with a happy heart!"

- Bargain "If you go to the store for me before noon, I will extend your curfew for the weekend."

1. Do you tend to be more optimistic and hopeful or more pessimistic and hopeless? Write down some examples that reflect either or both.

_____

_____

_____

_____

2. In general, when you communicate, do you stimulate a healthier, happier connection or cause discomfort and disconnection?

_____

_____

_____

_____

3. What styles of communication cause you to disconnect from the person you are with?

_____

_____

_____

_____

4. "When I need help around the house, I . . . (think of examples)

_____

_____

_____

_____ ."

5. "When things aren't going my way, I communicate my feelings about this by . . .

_____

_____

_____

_____ ."

Now, identify who you communicate most like:

1. "I communicate disappointment most like _____ .

   I communicate it by _____ ."

2. "I communicate love most like _____ .

   I communicate it by _____ ."

3. "I communicate fear/worry most like _____.

   I communicate it by _____ ."

4. "I communicate anger most like _____ .

   I communicate it by _____ ."

5. "I communicate disapproval most like _____.

   I communicate it by _____ ."

6. "I communicate mistakes I make most like _____.

   I communicate it by _____ ."

7. "I communicate happiness most like _____.

   I communicate it by _____ ."

8. "I communicate judgment most like _____.

   communicate it by _____ ."

9. "I communicate my needs most like _____ .

I communicate them by_____."

10. "I communicate how I feel about myself most like _____ .

I communicate it by _____ ."

Take a few moments and look over your list. What do you notice about how you are feeling or thinking in response to your observations? Reflect on any insights you may have.

_____

_____

_____

If this list made you aware of any negative emotions or self-judgment, then this is an excellent opportunity to practice being the Observer of these thoughts and feelings and extending compassion and acceptance to yourself.

☼
Exercise for Week 5, Days 2 and 3: Observing Your Communication Patterns
TIME ALLOCATION: MINDFULNESS MEDITATION FOR 15 MINUTES
SELF-OBSERVATIONS THROUGHOUT THE DAY
15 MINUTES OF REFLECTION.

Devote the next two days to being the Observer of your communication patterns. Take any insights about your communication style that you gained from exercise 1, and practice consciously observing your style in action. Throughout each day tune in to the voice of the Observer within you. Imagine the Observer saying things such as the following:

"Oh . . . look at that . . . I am judging just like (name the person)_____."

"Oh . . . look at that . . . I am speaking lovingly just like (name the person)_____."

Finish your day with the following reflective exercise:

1. Make a list of the characteristic ways you communicated throughout the day. (For example, "I observed that I criticized my child like my father criticized me.")

   A. _____

   B. _____

   C. _____

   D. _____

   E. _____

2. Identify the ways of communicating you would like to change.

3. Think of someone in your past or present whose ways of communicating you would like to emulate and guide you under similar circumstances. (For example, perhaps you liked the way your friend's mother listened and spoke to her children or others.)

   While holding a memory of this person, imagine yourself communicating like him or her during your parenting situations. Then use the space below to detail any specific changes you want to make in how you communicate. Remember to include both verbal and nonverbal components of communication, including word choice, tone of voice, facial expressions, and use of eyes, gestures, and behaviors.

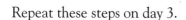

_____

_____

_____

Repeat these steps on day 3.

Exercise for Week 5, Day 4: The Four Gems of Communication
TIME ALLOCATION: MINDFULNESS MEDITATION FOR 20 MINUTES
OBSERVATIONS THROUGHOUT THE DAY
15 MINUTES OF REFLECTION.
Review: pages 169-173

Now that you are more aware of your communication patterns and you have a sense of the changes you want to make, the next four days are devoted to practice.

As you practice new communication styles, you can incorporate the *Four Gems of Communication*. Using these Four Gems will help you maintain and deepen the parent-child-connection and further reinforce the new style of communication you are working to establish.

Over the next four days follow the next few steps:

1) Schedule five minutes for yourself in the morning. Use this time to put your attention on your intention to incorporate the Four Gems into your daily interactions with your children. Spend several minutes sitting quietly and saying to yourself something like this:

"Today, I intend to . . . *listen first, be attentive, be expressive,* and *join with my children in their experiences.*"

2) Schedule ten minutes for reflective writing at the end of the day. Use this time to answer the following questions:

A. Did I have an opportunity to *listen first* before assuming I knew what my child was going to say? Was I attuned to myself? Was I attuned to my child? Did I communicate that I was listening? How did my child respond to this?

_____

_____

_____

_____

_____

B. Did I have an opportunity to *be attentive?* Was I attuned to myself? Was I attuned to my child? Did I communicate my attentiveness in some way?

_____

_____

_____

_____

C. Was I able to *be expressive?* What did I do to show my interest? How did I feel? How did my child respond to this? Did we seem more connected?

_____

_____

_____

_____

_____

D. Was I able to *join?* What did I do to show my child I was really involved in his world? How did I feel? How did my child respond to
this? Did we seem more connected?

_____

_____

_____

_____

Week 6: All Together Now

Objective: To integrate the Mindful Parent Happy Child program as a daily practice.

Dedicate this week to applying the new skills you have been learning in your daily mindful parenting practices. Whether you are in your home or out and about with children in tow, what you have been working on these past several weeks deserves additional review and reinforcement.

This final class will help you inject your new skills into daily interactions and activities with your children. As you go through the week, here is what you can expect:

• Each day you will have something to review at the beginning of the day and time for reflection at the end of the day. Give yourself about fifteen minutes for review and setting your intention.

- The format remains essentially the same each day, with a few minor variations. Make certain you read each question carefully, even though some questions are repeated.
- The number of evening reflection questions increases with each night. There are selected questions that are repeated. This repetition is essential to integration of your learning, so make sure you continue to answer these questions, even though it feels redundant.
- Each day includes ten minutes of Mindfulness Meditation. You can schedule this for any time that works well for you.

Engaging the Challenging Situation

Parents often find themselves accumulating situations that they avoid involving their children in, such as going shopping or eating in a restaurant. However, such occasions are actually wonderful opportunities to begin applying your new mindful parenting skills. So pull out the challenging situations you have been avoiding, and begin working with them. Let's go!

Write down at least four *difficult situations* you avoid in your parenting.

1.
2.
3.
4.

Next, look over your calendar. Plan a day when you are going to put yourself in each one of these difficult situations with your children. For example, your plan may look something like this:

Mon: *Go to grocery store with ____(name/s)____.*
Wed: *Go out to dinner with___(name/s)____.*
Thurs: *Bring ____(name/s)____ to the veterinarian.*
Sat: *Bring___(name/s)____to my hair appointment.*

Now that you know what you can expect from this week's class, and you know what days you will work with your difficult situations, you can begin organizing your schedule and setting your intention for a week of integrating the Mindful Parent Happy Child program into everyday life.

☀

Exercises for Week Six, Day 1:
TIME ALLOCATED: 35 MINUTES
10 MINUTES MINDFULNESS MEDITATION
15 MINUTES MORNING REVIEW
10 MINUTES REFLECTIVE WRITING

Morning Review
First Step:
Review the Class for week 1.

Second Step:
Look over your answers to the questions from class 1, exercise 3.

How many times a day do I pause to be mindfully aware?
What times of day am I likely to do this?
Where am I when I press the "pause button" the most?
What am I doing when I pause to observe?
What time of day was I inclined to journal and reflect?
Where is the best location for me to do reflective writing?

Once you have reviewed your answers, make necessary adjustments. Set your intention to press the "pause button" and be in moment-to-moment awareness with your whole self throughout the day. Use the Five Windows of Awareness as a guide.

Third Step:
Looking at your schedule, list the events in which you would like to be most mindful.

(Perhaps it is when your kids come home from school or when it's their bedtime.) Commit to two situations. If this is one of the days you bring in a difficult situation that you would prefer to avoid, include this as one of your choices.

1.
2.

Fourth Step:

Set your intention: "As a Mindful Parent my intention today is _____

_____ ."

Evening Reflection
First Step:

Sit quietly for a few minutes before you begin reflective writing. Allow your breath to slow you down until you become centered.

Second Step:

Answer the following questions in your notebook:

1. How many times did I press the "pause button" and take time for mindful awareness?
2. When I practiced mindful awareness, what changes or responses did I notice within me (i.e., mood, attitude, energy, pace)?
3. Was there anything different about how I felt going into the situations I chose?
4. Was there anything different about the way I parented?
5. Was there a situation I managed well? Describe?
6. Were there any moments of deeply felt connection between my children and me?
7. Were there times when I felt disconnected from my children?
8. Were there situations I would like to have handled differently?
9. Are there any unresolved issues to which I need to attend?
10. How am I feeling about my parenting right now?

Exercises for Week Six, Day 2:

Morning Review
First Step:
Review the phases of the MPHC model in class 3 and in chapter 3. Look over your responses to each exercise.

Second Step:
Review the acronym TINGLE on pages 129-134.

Third Step:
Look at your schedule. In what upcoming events would you like to be most mindful? Commit to two situations. If this is one of the days you bring in a difficult situation that you would prefer to avoid, include this as one of your choices.
    1.
    2.

Fourth Step:
    Set your intention: "As a Mindful Parent my intention today is _____

_____ ."

Evening Reflection
First Step:
Sit quietly for a few minutes before you begin reflective writing. Allow your breath to slow you down until you become centered.

Second Step:
Answer the following questions in your notebook.
    1. How many times did I press the "pause button" and take time for mindful awareness?

2. Did I find myself thinking about the phases of the MPHC model? When?

3. How did I integrate the MPHC model into my situations?

4. Was there an opportunity for me to do a self-intervention using the TINGLE method?

5. Did I have an opportunity for Deliberate Action?

6. What would I do differently?

7. Was there anything different from before in how the situations turned out?

8. Was there anything thing different in how my children responded?

9. Was there a situation in which I felt good about how I managed or responded?

10. Were there any moments of deeply felt connection between my children and me?

11. Were there times when I felt disconnected from my children?

12. Are there any unresolved issues I need to address?

13. How am I feeling about my parenting right now?

☀

Exercises for Week Six, Day 3

Morning Review
First Step:
Review class 2 to refresh yourself with the work you did on your family heirlooms. Also review your answers to the questions below that are found in exercise 3.

1. Have I gained any new insights?

2. What I like most about how I was parented is _____ .

3. The generational family patterns I want to keep are_____ .

4. The generational patterns I want to change are _____ .

Throughout the day, be the Observer of your family patterns, and remind yourself of the changes you want to make.

Second Step:

As you look over your schedule, list the times and places you would like to be most mindful. Commit to two situations where you will remind yourself to intentionally practice being mindful. If you select a day on which you have also scheduled a challenging situation with your children, make the challenging situation one of your choices.

1.
2.

Third Step:

Set your intention: "As a Mindful Parent my intention today is _____

_____ ."

Evening Reflection

First Step:

Sit quietly for a few minutes before you begin reflective writing. Allow your breath to slow down and deepen until you feel as calm and comfortable as possible.

Answer the following questions in your notebook.

1. How many times did I press the "pause button" and take time for mindful awareness?
2. When did I find myself thinking about the phases of the MPHC model?
3. How did I integrate the MPHC model into my situations?
4. Was there an opportunity for self-intervention using the TINGLE method?
5. Did I have an opportunity for Deliberate Action?
6. Looking back on my day, did I repeat any negative or positive family patterns?
7. As I operated more mindfully, did I do anything differently from my usual pattern?

8. Was there anything different in how my children responded?
9. Was there a situation I managed well?
10. Were there any moments of deeply felt connection between my children and me?
11. Were there times when I felt emotionally disconnected from my children?
12. Are there any unresolved issues to which I need to attend?
13. How am I feeling about my parenting right now?

Exercises for Week 6, Day 4

Morning Review
First Step:
Review chapter 3 and the classes for week 4.

Second Step:
Review your answers to the questions found in the exercises for week 6, days 2 and 3. Practice *living* the Three Principles as you integrate the MPHC model into your day.

Third Step:
Consult your schedule. What events are coming up that you believe are the best to consciously and purposefully practice mindfulness? Commit to two situations. Again, if this is one of the days you have chosen to engage a more challenging situation with your children—i.e., one that you would have previously tended to avoid—include this as one of your choices.

    1.
    2.

Fourth Step:
    Set your intention: "As a Mindful Parent my intention today is _____

_____ ."

Evening Reflection
First Step:
Sit quietly for a few minutes before you begin active reflection. Allow your breath to slow you down until you become centered.

Second Step:
Answer the following questions in your journal:
1. How many times did I press the "pause button" and take time for mindful awareness?
2. How did I apply the MPHC model in the situations I encountered?
3. What opportunities were present for me to do a self-intervention using the TINGLE method?
4. Did I take deliberate action to do something different from usual?
5. Did I allow the Three Principles of Mindful Parenting to guide me during the day?
6. What aspect of mindful parenting practice was the most difficult for me? Why?
7. What changes do I see in myself?
8. What changes do I see in my parent-child connections?
9. Did I make a difference in a child's life today?
10. What positive seeds did I sow today?
11. What negative seeds did I sow today?
12. Looking back on the day, what do I want to do differently?
13. Were there any moments of deeply felt connection between my children and me?
14. Were there times when I felt disconnected with my children?
15. Are there any unresolved issues I need to actively address?
16. How am I feeling about my parenting right now?

Exercises for Week 6, Day 5

Morning Review
First Step:
Review your answers to the exercises in chapter 4.

Second Step:
Answer the following questions:
- When have I experienced *attunement* in my relationships with others? Describe what the experience was like.

_____

_____

- When have I experienced empathy in my relationships with others? Describe what the experience was like.

_____

_____

Third Step:
Looking at your schedule, in what events do you want to be less reactive, less judgmental, and more mindful? Commit to practicing the Mindful Parenting model in two upcoming situations. Again, if this is one of the days you bring in a challenging situation with your children that you would have formerly preferred to avoid, include this as one of your choices:

_____

_____

Fourth Step:

Set your intention: "My intention for parenting more mindfully today is

_____

_____ ."

Evening Reflection
First Step:

Sit quietly for a few minutes before you begin reflective writing. Allow your breath to slow you down and until you become centered.

Second Step:

Answer the following questions in your notebook.

1. How many times did I pause to practice mindful awareness?
2. How did I incorporate the MPHC model into my situations?
3. Did I apply the TINGLE method or use Deliberate Action at any point?
4. Did I practice living all Three Principles in my day?
5. When was I most attuned with my children?
6. Was I responsive to the cues my child used when communicating with me?
7. How did I show empathy toward my children?
8. What changes do I see in my parent-child connections?
9. Did I make a difference in a child's life today?
10. What positive seeds did I sow today?
11. What negative seeds did I sow today?
12. What would I like to do differently?
13. Were there any moments of deeply felt connection between my children and me?
14. Was there a time when I felt less connected to my children?
15. Are there any unresolved issues I need to work on?
16. How am I feeling about my parenting right now?

Exercises for Week 6, Day 6

Morning Review
First Step:
Review class 5 and the *Five Mighty R's* and the acronym STONE in chapter 5, pages 148-173.

Second Step:
Answer the following:
- Do I use any of the excuses described on page 148-173 *Yes*   or   *No*
- What excuses have I used?

_____

_____ . ”

Third Step:
What scheduled events are coming up in which you would like to be most mindful? Commit yourself to being consciously and purposefully mindful during two of these events. Again, if this is one of the days you have chosen to engage in a challenging situation with your children, include this as one of your choices.

Fourth Step:
Set your intention: "As a Mindful Parent my intention today is _____

_____ . ”

Evening Reflection
First Step:
Sit quietly for a few minutes before you begin reflective writing. Slow and deepen your breath in order to slow you down until you feel more emotionally balanced and present in the moment.

Second Step:

Answer the following questions in your journal:

1. How many times did I pause to practice mindful awareness?
2. How did I incorporate the MPHC model into my day?
3. Did I use the TINGLE method or take Deliberate Action to do something different today?
4. Did I live all Three Principles today?
5. When was I most attuned with my children?
6. Was I responsive to my child's communication with me?
7. When did I show empathy toward my children?
8. What changes do I see in my parent-child connections?
9. Did I make a difference in a child's life today?
10. What positive seeds did I sow today?
11. What negative seeds did I sow today?
12. Which of the *Five Mighty R's* did I use today to connect with my children?
13. Did I use any of the excuses I identified earlier? Which ones?
14. Would I do anything differently?
15. Were there any moments of deeply felt connection between my children and me?
16. Were there times when I felt disconnected from my children?
17. Are there any unresolved issues in my parenting that need more work?
18. How am I feeling about my parenting right now?

Exercises for Week 6, Day 7

Morning Review
First Step:

Review the section "The Thirty-Second Connection" in chapter 5, page 173-174.

Second Step:

Answer the following question in your journal:

- What are the times of day when I can easily make a thirty-second connection?

_____

_____

Third Step:
In what upcoming scheduled events would you do well to practice mindfulness? Choose two situations in which you can do this consciously and with purpose. If you have already chosen a challenging situation with your children (i.e., one that you have normally tended to avoid), only choose one additional event.

    1.

    2.

Fourth Step:
Set your intention: "As a Mindful Parent my intention today is _____

_____ ."

Evening Reflection
First Step:
Sit quietly for a few minutes before you begin reflective writing. Allow your breath to slow you down until you become centered.

Second Step:
Answer the following questions in your journal:

1. How many times did I press the "pause button" and take time for mindful awareness?
2. How did I apply the MPHC model in situations I encountered?
3. Did I use the TINGLE method or Deliberate Action today?
4. Did I allow all Three Principles to guide my day?
5. When was I most attuned with my children?

6. Was I responsive to the cues my child used when communicating with me?
7. When did I display empathy toward my children?
8. What changes do I see in my parent-child connections?
9. Did I make a difference in a child's life today?
10. What positive seeds did I sow today?
11. What negative seeds did I sow today?
12. Which of the *Five Mighty R's* did I use today to connect with my children?
13. Did I use any of the excuses I identified earlier? Which ones?

"The primary path to a more compassionate mind is to focus on your ability to feel empathy."

Chapter Seven
The Seeds We Sow Become the Garden We Grow

"We are all in this together; if there is a role we can play
collectively to try to transform the world in some
positive way, it's time to begin."
–Dan Siegel

I magine this: You wake up, pour a cup of coffee, and tune in to your favorite news station. Here are some of the lead stories you hear:

"Teen Girl Reads to the Blind"
"A Michigan Truck Driver Saves Deer"
"Local Track Star Coaches Special Olympics"
"NFL Coach Volunteers at After-School Center"
"Executive Rallies Coworkers to Sing at Senior Centers"
"Banker Eats Lunch with Homeless"

"Neighborhood Grocer Gives Produce to Local Crisis House"
"Man Climbs Telephone Pole to Rescue Cat"

If you were to wake up to a radio broadcast with such positive and uplifting news items, it might seem as if the world had transformed itself while you were sleeping. But these are not the stories we are hearing, and the question is this: Why not?

Listening to Something Else

To develop our innate ability to be empathic and compassionate, we need to quiet the noise and fend off the distractions that weaken our well-being.

In the Disney movie *Land Before Time*, Mama Longneck tells her son Littlefoot a story about the Great Valley: a land she has heard described as lush, bountiful, and overflowing with food and running water; a land free from drought, floods, famine, and predation. Never having any real evidence of the actual existence of this Utopian place, Mama Longneck wisely explains to her inquiring son, "Some things you see with your eyes, while other things you see with your heart."

Even though Mama Longneck had never seen the Great Valley, she knew it existed because she chose to let her heart rule her sight. No matter what the outer world tries to tell us and sell us, compassionate acts exist at every street corner in every city and village; we just have to open our hearts and minds to observe them and pass them on.

At the same time, stimulating distractions infiltrate our daily lives, and in order to develop empathy and compassion, we have to be intentional about what we feed our minds. If we nourish our minds by focusing on compassion, we will literally be growing the empathy center of our brain. Intentionality is the key to cultivating the seeds of empathy and compassion within ourselves and in our relationships, and there are endless ways to accomplish it.

The primary path to a more compassionate mind is to focus on your ability to feel empathy. To develop our innate ability to be empathic and compassionate, we need to quiet the noise and fend off the distractions that weaken our well-being. A necessary first step is to remove ourselves from the media milieu of negative commentary. A lot of negative commentary comes at us from television, the Internet, and radio. Try an experiment. Give yourself a break from such commentary. Carve out the time and space necessary for your mind to become quieter, for your brain to be less "turned on." Here is my challenge to you: Unplug yourself.

Carve out the time and space necessary for your mind to become quieter, for your brain to be less "turned on."

EXERCISE

For one month do the following:

- Shut down the multiple conduits that connect you to the national and international news—television shows included.
- Keep a journal and record what you notice within yourself as you take this break from the news. You may find yourself feeling more or less restless or relieved.
- At the end of each week rate your mood level. Using five-point scales, record your subjective levels

of happiness, depression, peacefulness, and anxiousness.

- Each week observe and describe the quality of your mental activity. Explore any changes you notice related to what you think about throughout the day.
- At the end of the month, turn on the news and reconnect with the media outlets you customarily used. Write down what you notice within yourself when you resume.
- Journal about what this "news fast" has been like for you. Record any new awareness or understanding you may have about the effects of news commentary on your perspectives and ways of thinking.

If you typically engage in listening to or reading the news for twenty minutes a day or more, this will be a challenging exercise. At the end of thirty days you most likely will have experienced some interesting and different things. Journaling will allow you to bring to consciousness any changes in your experience and keep track of them.

When the month is over and you return to your normal routine of news media, use questions like the following to guide your reflection:

Since being engaged with news media once again

- How have my moods changed?
- How do I spend my time differently?
- Do I interact with my children differently?
- Do I go to bed at a different time?
- Am I more or less distracted?
- Am I more or less compassionate?

After completing this experiment, you will have a greater appreciation for the subtle ways news stories impact you. Likely there will be times when you are not consciously listening to the reports, but visual glimpses of the screen or feelings of intensity in a voice will influence your mood and ways of interacting with others. In order to stay focused on watering the positive seeds of thought and emotion within ourselves and in our children, we must guard against being overly exposed to the cruelty and violence of others. Don't cut yourself off from the world. Find the correct balance that will support your intention to be mindful every day. Purposefully include stories that touch your heart and cultivate your empathy and compassion.

The goal of the media industry is to grab us and hold our attention. Actually, much of the time it grabs us by the amygdala!

The goal of the media industry is to grab us and hold our attention. Actually, much of the time it grabs us by the amygdala!

Turn Down the Fear

Do you remember the Digging Deeper Box "Your Brain on Alert" (page 21)? Our primitive brain is designed to alert us to possible threats by releasing hormones—most notably, adrenaline and cortisol—that stimulate the fight, flight, or freeze response. Before our brain even has a chance to send this "threat" information to reasoning circuits of our brain, our body is told to react, and react big. Problems occur when we are unable to submit the "reaction mode" of the primitive brain to the regulated mode of the reasoning brain.

If we are told that terrorists might be living next door, or that the Sunday school teacher is a child molester, our brain triggers a fear reaction before we are able to process the information and reason things out critically. When we are flooded with news stories and we don't take time to differentiate what is true from what is amplified or exaggerated (for ratings), we experience an increased level of stress, which can contribute to an imbalance or illness in mind, body, and spirit.

The purpose of "unplugging" is to alleviate the persistent negative arousal that is streaming in from the background of life. We all need time to be quiet, still, and present in order to become awakened to the innate aspects of our humanity.

When my husband and I turned off our television, it took about a week before I stopped hearing snippets of news and seeing pictures of tragedy in my mind. I found myself missing my favorite news reporters, the ones who linked me to bad news around the world. Misery loves company, and the purveyors of news want your attention, even when you are made miserable by their reports!

After the negative echoes in my head ceased, I found myself thinking more creatively. I actually found that I had been craving opportunities to be creative. My mindfulness practice made me aware that I was more positive, and this produced a greater sense of well-being as I performed my day-to-day activities. I became more attuned with others and myself.

During my news fast, my husband and I were faced with several significant crises on the home front, yet I found myself embracing them with clarity, hopefulness, and resilience. My quieter mind was a beautiful, peaceful mirror of the world around me, enabling me to appreciate more deeply the sounds of the birds in my backyard and the hum of the bees kissing the basil flowers in my garden.

Here are a few other background distractions that you

The purpose of "unplugging" is to alleviate the persistent negative arousal that is streaming in from the background of life.

will want to pay attention to throughout your day. These may be found in conversations with coworkers, neighbors, teachers, committees, and all other interpersonal relationships, or in your own inner dialogue:

- listening to or participating in negative gossip
- making assumptions
- judgment (taking a "better than" or "less than" position)

Here is something to remember, and perhaps it can become a kind of mantra: *What we focus on becomes magnified, and what we magnify becomes real.*

From "I" to "We"

When I work with couples, I often offer a simple assignment for them to perform in my office. I ask each partner to make a list of the ways in which they contribute to the *"We"* in their relationship. When couples adjust to thinking and behaving toward their partner from the "We" perspective, they begin to perceive and understand each other's past behaviors in new ways. Each partner begins to grasp how being in a relationship as an "I" can impact their partner's sense of connection and well-being. When a couple shifts from thinking and living in the "I" to thinking and living as a "We," they open the door to perceiving channels to the heart, and a pathway is prepared for a sweet transformation.

A family in which each individual feels connected to each other is a family that functions as a "We." This is modeled by the parents' discernment of when to be living in the "I" (*autonomy and individuality*) and when to be living as

A family in which each individual feels connected to each other is a family that functions as a "We."

a "We" (*reliance and community*). Self-reflection, being the Observer of the self, allows us to see when we are being an "I" when it would be more unifying and empowering to be in the "We." The "I" is essential to maintaining our sense of self, to knowing who we are and the values and morals that are our personal compass. The community breaks down when the "I" becomes self-serving and ignores the needs of the "We."

Outside of the safety net of our home we are surrounded by "I"-oriented corporations, such as the morally insensitive Halliburton, which has recently paid out criminal fines of $382 million. Compare this company to Southwest Airlines—a more "We"-oriented company. Southwest has demonstrated that a corporate culture in which *employees are number 1* can make a company successful beyond its industry counterparts. Southwest Airlines is the only airline that did not lay off employees after the September 11th attacks. In fact, they opened their Norfolk location that same year. Today Southwest continues to thrive and open new locations while other airlines have either closed down or been bought out.

Which orientation do we, as citizens of the United States, see our government operating from? Every day our leaders must choose between voting as a "We," as in "We the people," and voting as an "I," as in responding to corporate lobbying. Perhaps we can all ask ourselves, "Do I vote as a 'We' or do I vote as an 'I'?" What would the difference be for you?

Let us consider the impact of an "I" orientation versus a "We" orientation in sharing our planet's natural resources. Ecologists who have studied the current and long-term impacts of global warming have suggested for decades that humans need to consume differently. A cultivated consciousness that works on this issue as a "We" is clearly a paradigm shift we need to make in order for our earth to return to its natural order.

Do you believe that your individual efforts at conservation won't make that much of a difference? If so, in one sense you are right. Your efforts *alone* won't make any real difference. However, this is reflective of an "I" way of thinking and seeing your place in the world community. Instead, shift your consciousness and practice your efforts in conservation as a "We." This mindset will strengthen the collective consciousness, and together we change the world.

If compassion were to become the newest epidemic, then we could knock out the infectious greed of the "I" and grow future "We" generations who will go further and work harder to respect, nourish, and sustain the delicate interplay between humans and nature.

In our work as a "We," we teach our children the deep interconnectedness we have to all living things, that as humans "we" are part of an integral web that we must respect and care for together. As parents, we model for our children a way of thinking and living more as a "We" than as an "I." We demonstrate this by how we treat each other and our planet. Eventually our efforts will pay off. Our children will be wired to build relationships as a "We." Our children will be more inclined to take care of our oceans, air, and land, and the habitats of migrating birds. The next time you wonder if using cloth grocery bags or unplugging your electronics at night really makes a difference, shift out of the "I" and into the "We." Remember that your children are mirroring and developing their "We" minds from your example.

The next time you wonder if using cloth grocery bags or unplugging your electronics at night really makes a difference, shift out of the "I" and into the "We."

Cultivating Compassion

Unfortunately, it often takes a catastrophe that involves human suffering and annihilation to arouse us to acts of compassion. Our busy lives stop momentarily as we stare at the devastated human lives on the television screen and respond with tears; we open our wallets and mail care packages stuffed with needed supplies. This reaction is appropriate and understandable, but this kind of compassion is often activated by media sources that have designed their messages for high emotional impact. To be a participant as a "We," we must water the seeds of compassion daily. Consistent compassion comes from within and is expressed during moments of attending and responding to others. Using *intention to cultivate compassion* promotes changes that can manifest far and wide.

As we intentionally seek out and cultivate compassion, we can use our minds to alter the physical structures of our brains and central nervous systems. Through mindfulness practices, we can learn to exercise compassion rather than react to situations using primitive fear responses. By intentionally focusing our attention on seeing things from an empathic and compassionate point of view, we invite our brain *to thicken* in this particular region. As we saw in the Introduction, this is the region of the brain that appears responsible for empathy, insight, attunement, bodily regulation, fear modulation, intuition, morality, and emotional balance (Siegel, 2007). Imagine a world in which the leaders of all nations were devoted to a mindfulness practice!

Let's begin with ourselves as parents. Buddhist monk Thich Nhat Hanh suggests that we water the seeds of compassion in ourselves and in others so that compassion will

As we intentionally

seek out and

cultivate

compassion, we

can use our minds

to alter the physical

structures of our

brains and central

nervous systems.

bloom like flowers. In the language of interpersonal neurobiology (Siegel, 2010), if you intentionally focus your mind on compassion, you wire a compassionate brain. Both of these wisdoms support the same idea: Compassion is a matter of intentional focus and self-cultivation.

Compassion Inspires

Our survival as a species relies upon something that is simultaneously basic and profound: compassion. In *The Empathic Civilization*, Jeremy Rifkin reinterprets human history, not in light of our lust for power and possessions but in terms of how compassion has shaped human development. He observes the following:

> "Recent discoveries in brain science and child development are forcing us to rethink the long-held belief that human beings are, by nature, aggressive, materialistic, utilitarian, and self-interested. The dawning realization that we are a fundamentally empathic species has profound and far-reaching consequences for society" (Rifkin, 2009).

With this realization, says Rifkin, the Age of Reason is beginning to give way to the Age of Empathy, perhaps just in time to save our planet, and ourselves.

Compassion has moved people to dive into freezing water to rescue an unlucky dog. Compassion motivates us to serve meals at homeless shelters and pluck stranded people off of rooftops during floods. Compassion is expressed when a stranger shows up to search for a lost child or when someone provides an abused animal a new home. Compassion is

Compassion is expressed when a stranger shows up to search for a lost child or when someone provides an abused animal a new home.

evident in the great teachings of Gandhi, Jesus, Mother Teresa, and the other sages and saints of history who devoted their lives to caring by performing actions of compassion.

Compassion can and must extend inward as well; compassion for ourselves correlates with our capacity for compassion toward others. As a parent, practicing self-compassion is essential to being compassionate toward your children, and it does require us to look inward. Deep, comprehensive self-compassion does not come easily for most of us, but it can be encouraged in the emotional work we do, the work that helps us make sense out of our lives.

Deep, comprehensive self-compassion does not come easily for most of us, but it can be encouraged in the emotional work we do, the work that helps us make sense out of our lives.

Looking inward and attending to ourselves with empathy and compassion creates health and stability, inspiring us to become better adults and parents. When we learn to account for and accept the many factors that have combined to make us who we are at this moment—as an individual, partner, and parent—we have an opportunity to cultivate greater compassion for those who took care of us when we were children. We can look at the trials, circumstances, and errors of our caretakers from an entirely different vantage point. We can feel empathy for them in a manner that will override anger and betrayal.

Having a more empathic and compassionate point of view does not mean that old feelings will never resurface; nor does it mean that past mistreatment is okay. It does mean that when feelings and memories of violation surface, we are able to engage them from a place of mental and emotional equilibrium that is characterized primarily by understanding. Research shows us that children whose parents have taken time out to gain self-understanding will themselves raise healthier, more securely attached children.

When we nourish compassion within ourselves, this

gives rise to more compassion within and among us, which enables empathy to multiply and spread like newly released seeds from a dandelion. Every day we have countless opportunities to make a conscious choice to engage ourselves and others empathically, watering the seeds of compassion.

The Power of Our Connection

In my life I am lucky to know people who inspire me to water the good seeds. In response, I consider it my mission and moral obligation to continue the process. As you look into your history, you may recollect people who have nourished you. As you and I cultivate our good seeds, think of all we can accomplish individually and collectively.

In their book *Connected*, Nicholas Christakis and James Fowler explain, "The science of social networks provides a distinct way of seeing the world because it is about individuals *and* groups, and about how the former actually becomes the latter" (2009). Christakis and Fowler's study on the effects of social networks led them to conceptualize the *Three Degrees of Influence Rule*.

This rule holds that "we influence and are influenced by people up to three degrees removed from us, most of whom we do not even know." In other words, the things I think, feel, and do affect not just my friend, but my friend's friend's friend.

The Three Degrees rule applies to a broad spectrum of personal and social phenomena, including political viewpoints, weight gain, suicide clusters, wealth or lack thereof, substance abuse, and happiness. It seems that what we think, feel, and do influences those around us. This influ-

Did You Know

Did You Know? If you know someone who is happy, this makes you 15.3 percent more likely to be happy yourself. And get this: A happy friend of a friend makes you 9.8 percent likely to be happy. Even your neighbor's sister's friend can give you a 5.6 percent boost (Christakis, 2009).

ence extends beyond our immediate family and friends to their friends and family.

The Three Degrees of Influence Rule provides part of the rationale for the first principle of the *Mindful Parent Happy Child* program, namely: *All adults are parents.* If you adopt and live this principle and you see yourself as part of a human community that is responsible for raising children—regardless of whether those children are related to you by blood, legal adoption, or work—you will increase your potential to be a positive influence in the world. Your family will observe you; your friends will be touched by you; and strangers will be influenced by you as you attend to the care and needs of a child, any child. The Three Degrees of Influence Rule gives us a new way of looking at how the empathy and compassion we sow influence the lives of children growing in our communal garden.

Why Mindful Parenting Matters

Poet William Ross Wallace said, "The hand that rocks the cradle rules the world." I prefer to think of it like this: "The hand that rocks the cradle *changes* the world."

A commitment to raising children well—and raising *well* children—is the moral and spiritual responsibility of every man and woman, if our species and our environment are going to survive and thrive. Shaping each individual child's life through effective parenting, teaching, and mentoring is the foundation of our collective social well-being.

Parents are stewards of their children's minds and hearts. Moms and dads do more than take care of their children's bodies and physical needs; they also support the

The Three Degrees of Influence Rule gives us a new way of looking at how the empathy and compassion we sow influence the lives of children growing in our communal garden.

development of a higher consciousness—a child's capacity for attunement, connectivity, empathy, compassion, and altruism. When the connection between children and their caretaking adults is safe, stable, and supportive, those children are more likely to develop into happier and healthier parents, employees, and citizens one day. Ultimately, the destiny of future generations depends on the quality of connection adults develop and maintain with the children of today.

The research is clear: Healthy patterns of self-discipline, emotional and social intelligence, mental health, and productivity are passed on from healthy adults to the children in their care. Similarly, unhealthy patterns of selfishness, abuse, addiction, and disorders of thought and emotion also are transmitted from one generation to the next.

Which patterns are transmitted and how they are transmitted begins not with the child but with you, the adult. If you are anxious, disorganized in your thinking, emotionally reactive, or physically abusive, the children in your care will likely develop and pass on similar patterns of personality and temperament. The responsibility to cultivate healthy patterns that will best shape future generations clearly begins with the adults.

Here is the good news: Research has also demonstrated that whatever your personal blend of "nature and nurture," and in spite of a troubled genetic heritage or adverse childhood experiences, these beliefs and experiences need not be the most significant determinants of your destiny. Habits of anxiety, reactivity, depression, and low self-esteem can compromise your ability to actively, healthfully engage in life and parenthood.

Through conscious, sustained effort, you can positively

Did You Know

Genes can't be changed in us, but they can change in their expression. In other words, our genes can be altered by our environment.

and constructively transform such inherited and socialized patterns.

This effort requires, first and foremost, that you learn to pay attention to yourself. Self-awareness is the first step to meaningful and lasting change. This is the path that will guide you to different ways of inward being and new patterns of outward response to the life events that unfold around you. This is the path that will lead you toward more mindful parenting—a gift to you, your child, and the future.

Call to Action: The Movement

The world needs to change. We cannot continue living reactively and selfishly and expect to survive. The solution to this problem begins with, and within, each of us. A positive outcome will not be realized if we fail to practice and promote ideas (such as the ones in this book) to those close to us and in our communities.

As I continue to study the problems of children, families, and social groups, the focus of my intention becomes clearer. Our shared mission must be to cultivate mindful parenting in the consciousness of all adults, beginning with parents, teachers, mentors, and child care workers. In educational and publishing circles, there is currently an explosion of information about parenting. I like to imagine that a collective consciousness is working for the same cause. Parents matter in growing joyful, resilient, healthy, happy, kind, and sensitive children—and all adults play an important role. The minds, hearts, and hands we use to raise our children will shape their future for generations to come.

The task of generating a mindful parenting movement

What greater gift can we give our children and the future of our world than the cause of well-being?

does not need to overwhelm us, nor is the *Mindful Parent Happy Child* program the only valid approach to mindful parenting. Many programs use mindfulness in their teachings without ever mentioning the word "mindful." A mindful parenting movement requires your intention, energy, and commitment. It unifies us with a purpose.

Mindful parenting is more than an intellectual position or set of beliefs. It represents a comprehensive way of living and approaching life. What greater gift can we give our children and the future of our world than the cause of well-being? Movements of this sort can have more impact than a passing trend; they have the potential to alter our ways of being and becoming into something more salutary, relevant, and permanent.

To generate the spirit of a mindful parenting movement, follow any one of the suggestions listed below. As you choose a course of action to follow, consider the people and layers of connection you will influence with a little intention.

Suggestions:
1. *Wear it:* You can display your commitment to the Mindful Parenting Movement by ordering a license plate holder for your car or motorcycle. What effect would it have on you if you saw at least one license plate holder a day that read: "Another Mindful Parent" or "Mindful Mom on Board" or "Mindful Dad, Happy Children"? How might this affect your parenting that day? Do you think you would become more mindful, more centered with yourself, and maybe more available to your children? Would such a reminder help you to drive more safely or to more

Mindful

parenting is

more than an

intellectual

position or set

of beliefs. It

represents a

comprehensive

way of

living and

approaching

life.

consciously prepare yourself to be a better parent at the end of the workday as you transform from being a boss or employee to being a family member?

2. *Become a class facilitator*: Start your own Mindful Parenting class in your neighborhood, religious organization, school, or clinical practice. Become a certified Mindful Parent Happy Child Facilitator. (For mental health professionals, Continuing Education credits are available. For more information, visit www.mindfulparenthappychild.com.)

3. *Host a class*: When you host a class or day retreat for ten people or more, you can get the class for free. The fee depends on the number of people in the group.

4. *Invite a trained facilitator to speak*: As the number of trained *Mindful Parent Happy Child* facilitators increases, presenters will become more available to speak at schools, PTAs, parent groups, and other appropriate venues.

Those of us who are committed to Mindful Parenting would love to hear your ideas on how we can sustain and build this movement together as it spreads around the world. For now, we hope you find this a useful resource to use and share with others. You are on a path that inspires and transforms.

These are my wishes for you: May you find deep joy as a parent. May the connection you have with your child be everlasting, fulfilling, and always growing. May your mindful parenting spread like the seeds of a dandelion.

Quick Glance: Chapter Seven

Listening to Something Else

- No matter what the outer world tries to tell us and sell us, compassionate acts exist at every street corner in every city and village; we just have to open our hearts and minds to observe them and pass them on.

- If we nourish our minds by focusing on compassion, we will literally be growing the empathy center of our brain. Intentionality is the key to cultivating the seeds of empathy and compassion within ourselves and in our relationships, and there are endless ways to accomplish it.

Turn Down the Fear

- When we are flooded with news stories and we don't take time to differentiate what is true from what is amplified or exaggerated (for ratings), we experience an increased level of stress, which can contribute to an imbalance or illness in mind, body, and spirit.

- The purpose of "unplugging" is to alleviate the persistent negative arousal that is streaming in from the background of life. We all need time to be quiet, still, and present in order to become awakened to the innate aspects of our humanity.

From "I" to "We"

- A family in which each individual feels connected to each other is a family that functions as a "We." This is modeled by the parents' internal experience of discerning when to be living in the "I" (*autonomy and individuality*) and when to be living as a "We" (*reliance and community*).

- The "I" is essential to maintaining our sense of self, to knowing who we are and the values and morals that are our personal compass. The community breaks down when the "I" becomes self-serving and ignores the needs of the "We."

- As parents, we model for our children a way of thinking and living more as a "We" than as an "I." We demonstrate this by how we treat each other and our planet. Eventually our efforts will pay off. Our children will be wired to build relationships as a "We." Our children will be more inclined to take care of our oceans, air, and land, and the habitats of migrating birds.

Cultivation Compassion

- To be a participant as a "We," we must water the seeds of compassion daily. Consistent compassion comes from within and is expressed during moments of attending and responding to others. Using *intention* to *cultivate compassion* promotes changes that can manifest far and wide.

Compassion Inspires

- Looking inward and attending to ourselves with empathy and compassion creates health and stability, inspiring us to become better adults and parents. When we learn to account for and accept the many factors that have combined to make us who we are at this moment—as an individual, partner, and parent—we have an opportunity to cultivate greater compassion for those who took care of us when we were children.

The Power of Our Connection

- *Three Degrees of Influence Rule*: This rule holds that "we influence and are influenced by people up to three degrees removed from us, most of whom we do not even know." In other words, the things I think, feel, and do affect not just my friend, but my friend's friend's friend.

Why Mindful Parenting Matters

- The research is clear: Healthy patterns of self-discipline, emotional and social intelligence, mental health, and productivity are passed on from healthy adults to the children in their care.

- Habits of anxiety, reactivity, depression, and low self-esteem can compromise your ability to actively, healthfully engage in life and parenthood. Through conscious, sustained effort, you can positively and constructively transform such inherited and socialized patterns.

"Practice acceptance and nonjudgment; there is no right or wrong way to being in the present."

Acknowledgements

Before writing this book I went to the "writers" section of my favorite bookstore to search for something that would help me brush-up on my writing skills. Mary Pipher's book *Writing to Change the World* immediately caught my attention; I knew making a contribution to better the world would be my primary purpose in writing this book. Her words often came to mind as I wrote:

> *"Writing to connect is "change writing," which, like good therapy, creates the conditions that allow people to be transformed."*
> —M. Pipher, 2006

It remains to be seen if I will accomplish my larger purpose, however I do know one thing for certain—writing this book has been transformational for me. Along the way I have asked many people for big favors. I learned to lean on friends, family and colleagues when I needed help, and relied upon them much more than my normally independent spirit would have formerly allowed. I have discovered, for me at least, that a book cannot be written by one person—it takes a village.

Now I am glad to have arrived at a time and place where I can thank all those who have given me so much. My heart is full of gratitude and appreciation as I do so. Some of these special people cheered me on, read chapters and gave me feedback. Some held me up through a terrifically challenging year. Some edited and proofread the text, correcting spelling, grammar, syntax, and helpfully placing semi-colons and em dashes where needed.

I thank my husband Frank, who spent hours editing the rough pages of my early draft and insisted on being there for the final polishing touches. His wordsmithing helped make complex concepts easier to understand; he often took my ideas and elucidated them with fluidity, refinement, and simplicity. His loving acceptance and support continues to inspire me to be present, to accept change, and become more mindful.

I thank my parents, Richard and Jeanne Placone. Their fierce love for our family, and their generosity of time, service and resources in helping others—including their aid and support of me with this project—is what will always inspire me to be a better person. My sister Alicia encouraged me in just the right way, and at the right times, as only a good sister can do. I thank my brother Rick and his wife Chela for opening their lovely Napa home to me when I needed a place to retreat to and write. I am grateful to my sisters-in-law Donna and Helen for giving me "two-thumbs-up" after reading my work, and to my step-children, Ian and Claire for inspiring me to love more broadly and deeply. To all my in-laws, Nell, Steve, Elaine and Tom: your kind words were felt and cherished. For my nephews and nieces and all the love they shared with me along the way, my appreciation is unending.

My deepest gratitude is reserved for my Anam Cara Sisters: Pam, Maura, Liza, and Yvonne. Our gatherings have been a spiritual "tether" in my life. They always bring me back to center, not only by their words, but also by how they continue to model life-paths grounded in serenity and peace, love and joy, courage and integrity, strength and gumption.

A very special thanks to my Cheerleading Squad—for the many ways in which they nurtured my vision and kept me focused: Linda Brown-Key, Pat and Mark Bryning, Carolyn Biglow, Felena Hanson, Andrea Schneider, Gina Simmons, Lynn Feinberg, Suzan Tusson, Lynn Wight, and the dynamic women in my first Mindful Moms Group: Mallory, Julie, Katy, Michelle, Mahrya, Misha and Diane.

I especially want to thank Dr. Kai MacDonald who graciously contributed the text for one of the "Delving Deeper" boxes, and made sure I was correctly representing the neuroscience related to mindfulness and attachment. Any errors that might remain are completely my responsibility. Also I deeply appreciate those who generously went through the manuscript and gave valuable input: Tina MacDonald, R.N., Diane Slagle, Toni Rogers, Shannon Wallace, Cindy Camberg, and Sherry Hartwell.

A special thanks is also extended to Dr. Ruth P. Newton, for the time she took in writing the forward, and for the suggestions and support she gave to the entire project.

Thanks to my editor, Nesta Aharoni, who probably thought the writing and rewriting would never end, yet graciously accepted multiple revisions for review. Her belief in this project gave me the confidence to bring it to completion. And thank you, Vicki Boyle, for the efficient and thorough job of indexing.

I want to thank all of the children who attended the photo shoot for the cover of this book, and for the parents who got them there. Photographer Michael P. Franklin, I thank you for your big heart and your valuable time. Your ability to work with a room full of squirmy children was truly amazing; because of you, their big smiles were authentic and sincere.

Finally, a huge "thank you" is reserved for those who transformed my manuscript into the very book I initially envisioned. The team at CenterPointe Media has been incredible; their professionalism and punctuality unwavering—I have the deepest respect for this excellent company and its staff, especially Joan's keen eyes for detail and design. Foremost, I want to say thanks to Matthew (the gem) Greenblatt who directed me ever so gently through each step, and who always remained positive as deadlines passed me by. His kind nature and professional demeanor made me happy and ever ready to engage him in countless phone consultations and e-mails.

—Pilar M. Placone, Ph.D.

Notes

[1] Resnick, M. D. (1997)
[2] Baer et al. (2006)
[3] Bowlby, J. (1988)
[4] Schore, A. (1997; 2003)
[5] Belsky, J. and Fearon, R. M. (2002)
[6] Fonagy, P. and Target, M. (2005)

Delving Deeper: Oxytocin: The Bonding Hormone

[1] MacDonald, K. and MacDonald, T. M. (2010)
[2] Kosfeld, M. et al. (2005)
[3] Zak, P. J., Stanton, A. A. and Ahmadi, S. (2007)
[4] Guastella, A. J., Mitchell, P. B. and Dadds, M. R. (2008)
[5] Fischer-Shofty, M. et al. (2010)
[6] Hurlemann, R. et al. (2010)

[7] Bartz, J. A. et al. (2010)
[8] Shamay-Tsoory, S. G. et al. (2009)
[9] Mikolajczak, M. et al. (2010)
[10,] Snowdon, C. T. et al. (2010)
[11] Ross, H. E. et al. (2009)
[12] Beery, A. K., Lacey, E. A. and Francis, D. D. (2008)
[13] Feldman, R. et al. (2007)
[14] Feldman, R. et al. (2010)
[15] Naber, F. et al. (2010)
[16] Gordon, I. et al. (2010)
[17] Meinlschmidt, G. and Heim, C. (2007)
[18] Riem, M. M. et al. (2010).
[19] Strathearn, L. et al. (2009).
[20] Tanaka, K., Osako, Y. and Yuri, K. (2010)
[21] Champagne, F. A. (2008)
[22] Carter, C. S. (2005)
[23] Heim, C. et al. (2009)
[24] Pierrehumbert, B. et al. (2010)
[25] Buchheim, A. et al. (2009)

Delving Deeper: Your Brain on Alert

[1] Murray, E. (2007)
[2] Cannon, W. B. (1915)
[3] Atkinson R. L. et al. (1996), Kandal, E. R. and Schwartz, H. (1992)
[4] Schore, A. (1997)
[5] Yi-Yuan T. et al. (1997)

Delving Deeper: You Can Change Your Brain

[1] Garland, E. L. and Howard, M.O. (2009)
[2] Goldin, P. R. and Gross, J. (2010)
[3] Ramel, W. G. et al. (2004)
[4] Chiesa, A. A. and Serretti, A. (2009)
[5] Davidson, R. et al. (2003)
[6] Cahn & Polich (2006), Jha, A. P. et al. (2007)
[7] Jha, et al. (2010)
[8] Yi-Yaun T. et al. (2009)

Delving Deeper: Highlighting Implicit Memory

[1] Siegel, D. J. (1999)
[2] Badenoch, B. (2008)

Delving Deeper: Attachment and The Parent-Child Connection

[1] Bowlby, J. (1988)
[2] Newton (2008)
[3] Siegel, D. J., Hartzell, M. (2003)
[4] Main, M. A. (1990)

Delving Deeper: The Nature of Mind

Siegel, D. J. (1999, 2010)

Delving Deeper: Marvelous Mirror Neurons

[1] Singer, T. (2004)
[2] Iacoboni, M. et al. (2005)
[3] Ramachandran, V. (2006)

References

Ainsworth, M. B. (1978). *Patterns of Attachment: A Psychological Study of the Strange Situation*. Hillsdale, NJ, Erlbaum.

Atkinson, R. L. (1996). *Hilgard's Introduction to Psychology*. (12th ed.). Fort Worth, Harcourt Brace College Publishers.

Badenoch, B. (2008). *Being a Brain-Wise Therapist: A Practical Guide to Interpersonal Neurobiology*. New York, W. W. Norton & Company.

Bartz, J. A. et al. (2010). *Oxytocin Selectively Improves Empathic Accuracy*. Published online before print. Psychological Science. Accessed September, 10, 2010.

Bear, R. et al. (2006). *Using Self-Report Assessment Methods to Exploring Facets of Mindfulness*. Journal of Cognitive Neuroscience 18:871-79.

Beery, A. K., Lacey, E. A. and Francis, D. D. (2008). *Oxytocin and Vasopressin Receptor Distributions in a Solitary and a Social Species of Tuco-Tuco (Ctenomys Haigi and Ctenomys Sociabilis)*. The Journal of Comparative Neurology 507:6, 1847-59.

Belsky, J. and Pasco Fearon, R. M. (2002). *Infant–Mother Attachment Security, Contextual Risk, and Early Development: A Moderational Analysis*. Development and Psychopathology 14:293-310.

Berger, P. (1967). *The Sacred Canopy: Elements of a Sociological Theory of Religion*. New York, Anchor Books.

Biddulph, S. (2002). *The Secret of Happy Children: Why Children Behave the Way They Do—and What You Can Do to Help Them to Be Optimistic, Loving, Capable and Happy*. New York, Marlowe & Company.

Bowen, M. M. (1978). *Family Therapy in Clinical Practice*. Northvale, NJ, Jason Aronson.

Bowlby, J., Robertson, J., and Rosenbluth, D. (1952). *A Two-Year-Old Goes to Hospital*. Psychoanalytical Study of the Child 7,82-94.

Bowlby, J. (1988). *A Secure Base: Clinical Applications of Attachment Theory*. London, Routledge.

Bowlby, J. (1988). *A Secure Base: Parent-Child Attachment and Healthy Human Development*. New York, Basic Books.

Bowlby, J. (1969, 1982). *Attachment and Loss: Volume 1, Attachment*. New York, Basic Books.

Buchheim, A. et al. (2009). *Oxytocin Enhances the Experience of Attachment Security*. Psychoneuroendocrinology 34:9, 1417-22.

Cannon, W. B. (1915, 1963). *Bodily Changes in Pain, Hunger, Fear and Rage.* New York, Harper.

Carmody, J. A. (2008). *Relationships Between Mindfulness Practice and Levels of Mindfulness, Medical and Psychological Symptoms and Well-Being in a Mindfulness-Based Stress Reduction Program.* Journal of Behavioral Medicine 3:1, 23-33.

Carter, C. S. (2005). *The Chemistry of Child Neglect: Do Oxytocin and Vasopressin Mediate the Effects of Early Experience?* Proceedings of the National Academy of Sciences 102:51, 18247-8.

Champagne, F. A. (2008). *Epigenetic Mechanisms and the Transgenerational Effects of Maternal Care.* Front Neuroendocrinol 29:3, 386-97.

Cheng, H., Furnham, A. (2004). *Perceived Parental Rearing Style, Self-Esteem and Self-Criticism as Predictors of Happiness.* Journal of Happiness Studies 5:1, 1-21.

Chiesa, A. A. and Serretti, A. (2009). *Mindfulness-Based Stress Reduction for Stress Management in Healthy People: A Review and Metanalysis.* Journal of Alternative and Complementary Medicine 15:5, 593-600.

Damasio, A. (1999). *The Feeling of What Happens: Body and Emotion in the Making of Consciousness.* San Diego, Harcourt.

Davidson, R. (2003). *Alterations in Brain and Immune Functions Produced by Mindfulness Meditation.* Psychosomatic Medicine 65:564-570.

Dobbs, D. (2006). *A Revealing Reflection.* Scientific American Mind 17:2, 22-27.

Duncan, L. G. (2009). *A Model of Mindful Parenting: Implications for Parent-Child Relationships and Prevention*

Research. Clinical Child and Family Psychology Review 12:3, 255-70.

Feldman, R. et al. (2007). *Evidence for a Neuroendocrino-logical Foundation of Human Affiliation: Plasma Oxytocin Levels Across Pregnancy and the Postpartum Period Predict Mother-Infant Bonding.* Psychological Science 18:11, 965-70.

Feldman, R. et al. (2010). *Natural Variations in Maternal and Paternal Care are Associated with Systematic Changes in Oxytocin Following Parent-Infant Contact.* Psychoneuro-endocrinology 35:8, 1133-41.

Fischer-Shofty, M. et al. (2010). *The Effect of Intranasal Ad-ministration of Oxytocin on Fear Recognition.* Neuropsy-chologia 48:1, 179-84.

Fonagy, P. and Target, M. (2005). *Bridging the Transmission Gap: An End to Important Attachment Research?* Attach-ment & Human Development 7:3, 333-43.

Fredrickson, B. L. (2008). *Open Hearts Build Lives: Positive Emotions, Induced Through Loving-Kindness Meditation, Build Consequential Personal Resources.* Journal of Per-sonality and Social Psychology 95:5, 1045-62.

Garcia-Pratts, C. (1997). *Good Families Don't Just Happen: Lessons We Learned Raising Our Ten Sons.* Holbrook, MA, Adams Media.

Garland, E. L., and Howard, M. O. (2009). *Neuroplasticity, Psychosocial Genomics, and the Biopsychosocial Paradigm in the 21st Century.* Health & Social Work 34:3, 191-99.

Goldin, P. R., Gross, J. (2010). *Effects of Mindfulness-Based Stress Reduction (MBSR) on Emotion Regulation in Social Anxiety Disorder.* Emotion 10:1, 83-91.

Goldstein, J. (1994). *Insight Meditation: The Practice of Freedom*. Boston, Shambhala Publishing.

Gordon, I., Zagoory-Sharon, O., Leckman J. F., Feldman R. (2010). *Oxytocin, Cortisol, and Triadic Family Interactions*. Physiology and Behavior 105, 678-84.

Gray, P. (2010). *The Dramatic Rise of Anxiety and Depression in Children and Adolescents: Is it Connected to the Decline in Play and Rise in Schooling?* Psychology Today. Retrieved from www.psychologytoday.com

Greenland Kaiser, S. (2010). *The Mindful Child: How to Help Your Kid Manage Stress and Become Happier, Kinder, and More Compassionate*. New York, Free Press.

Greenspan, S. I. (1997). *The Growth of the Mind and the Endangered Origins of Intelligence*. Reading, MA, Perseus Books.

Guastella, A. J., Mitchell, P. B., and Dadds, M. R. (2008). *Oxytocin Increases Gaze to the Eye Region of Human Faces*. Journal of the Society of Biological Psychiatry 63:1, 3-5.

Haidt, J. (2006). *The Happiness Hypothesis: Finding Modern Truth in Ancient Wisdom*. New York, Basic Books.

Hallowell, E. M. (1997). *The Childhood Roots of Adult Happiness: Five Steps to Help Kids Create and Sustain Lifelong Joy*. New York, Ballantine.

Hallowell, E. M. (1999). *Connect: 12 Vital Ties that Open Your Heart, Lengthen Your Life, and Deepen Your Soul*. New York, Pocket Books.

Hanson, P. (2007). *The Joy of Stress: How to Make Stress Work for You*. Riverside, NJ, Andrews McMeel Publishing.

Harlow, H. F. (1958). *The Nature of Love*. American Psychologist 13, 673-85.

Harlow, H. F., and Harlow, M. K. (1962). *Social Deprivation in Monkeys.* Scientific America 207:136-46.

Harlow, H. F., Zimmermann, R. (1996). *Affectional responses in the infant monkey.* Foundations of Animal Behavior xiv, 843, 376-387.

Haimowitz, M. L. and Haimowitz, N. R. (1966). *Human Development.* New York: Thomas Y. Crowell.

Healing Millions (2009). Search for: *Bodhisattva in Metro,* Retrieved April 2009 from www.youtube.com

Hebb, D. O. (1949). *The Organization of Behavior: A Neuro-Psychological Theory.* New York, Wiley.

Heim, C. et al. (2009). *Lower CSF Oxytocin Concentrations in Women with a History of Childhood Abuse.* Molecular Psychiatry 14:10, 954-8.

Horn, A. F. (2008). *Psychotherapy with Infants and Young Children: Repairing the Effects of Stress and Trauma on Early Attachment.* New York, Guilford Press.

Hurlemann, R. et al. (2010). *Oxytocin Enhances Amygdala-dependent, Socially Reinforced Learning and Emotional Empathy in Humans.* Journal of the Society for Neuroscience 30:14, 4999-5007.

Iacoboni M. et al. (2005). *Grasping the Intentions of Others with One's Own Neuron System.* PloS Science Biology 3:3, e 79.

Jetvig, S. (2007). *Drinking Water to Maintain Good Health.* Accessed March 15, 2007 from nutrition.about.com/od/hydrationwater/a/waterarticle.html

Jha, A. K. et al. (2007). *Mindfulness Training Modifies Subsystems of Attention. Cognitive,* Affective and Behavioral

Neuroscience 7:2, 109-19.

Johnson, D. (n.d.). *Resiliency in Health Care.* Retrieved 2010 from lessons4living.com: Resliency Training: www.lessons4living.com/healthcare_resiliency.htm

Johnson, S. (2008). *Hold Me Tight: Seven Conversations for a Lifetime of Love.* New York, Little, Brown and Company.

Kabat-Zinn, J. (1994). *Wherever You Go, There You Are.* New York, Hyperion.

Kabat-Zinn, M. A. (1997). *Everyday Blessings: The Inner Work of Mindful Parenting.* New York, Hyperion.

Kabat-Zinn, J. A. (1998). *Mindful Parenting.* From Yes! A Journal of Positive Futures. Accessed March 31, 1998 from www.yesmagazine.org/issues/millennium-survival-guide/mindful-parenting

Kabat-Zinn, J. (2003). *Mindfulness-Based Interventions in Context: Past, Present and Future.* Clinical Psychology: Science and Practice 10:2, 144-56.

Kabat-Zinn, J. (2004). *Coming to Our Senses.* New York, Hyperion Press.

Kandel, E. R. and Schwartz, H. (1992). *Principles of neural science,* 2nd ed. New York, Elsevier.

Kerr, M. E. (2005). *One Family's Story: A Primer on Bowen Theory.* Washington, D.C.: Bowen Center for the Study of Family, Georgetown Family Center.

Kornfield, J. (1993). *A Path With Heart.* New York, Bantam Books.

Kornfield, J. (2007). *Omega Awakening the Best in the Human Spirit.* Retrieved from http://eomega.org/omega/faculty/viewProfile/e87c2a6f0fab038dc4f158e76c76654e/

Kornfield, J. (2009). *The Wise Heart.* New York, Bantam Books.

Kosfeld, M. et al. (2005). *Oxytocin Increases Trust in Humans.* Nature 435:7042, 673-6.

Krishnamurti, J. (1996). *Total Freedom: The Essential Krishnamurti.* New York, Harper.

Lantieri, L. and Goleman, D. (2008). *Building Emotional Intelligence: Techniques to Cultivate Inner Strength in Children.* Boulder, CO: True Sounds. (Daniel Goleman wrote introduction and presented exercises for CD.)

Lozowick, L. (1997). *Conscious Parenting.* Prescott, AZ, Hohm Press.

MacDonald, K. and MacDonald, T. M. (2010). *The Peptide that Binds: A Systematic Review of Oxytocin and its Prosocial Effects in Humans.* Harvard Review of Psychiatry 18:1, 1-21.

Main, M. A. (1990). *Procedures for Identifying Infants as Disorganized/Disoriented During the Ainsworth Strange Situation.* In M. G. D. Chichetti and E. M. Cummings (Ed.), *Attachment in the Preschool Years.* Chicago: University of Chicago Press.

Maxwell, J. C. (2003). *Thinking for a Change: 11 Ways Highly Successful People Approach Life and Work.* New York, Center Street.

Meinlschmidt, G. and Heim, C. (2007). *Sensitivity to Intranasal Oxytocin in Adult Men with Early Parental Separation.* Biological Psychiatry 61:9, 1109-11.

Mikolajczak, M. et al. (2010). *Oxytocin Makes People Trusting, Not Gullible.* Psychological Science, Sage Journals Online.

Miller, A. (1979). *The Drama of the Gifted Child.* New York, Van Nostrand Reinhold.

Murray, E. (2007). *The Amygdala, Reward and Emotion*. Elsevier; Trends in Cognitive Sciences 11:11, 489-97.

Nhat Hanh, T. (1994). *The Miracle of Mindfulness*. Boston, Beacon Press.

Nhat Hanh, T. (1996). *Being Peace*. Berkeley, Parallax Press.

Naber, F. et al. (2010). *Intranasal Oxytocin Increases Fathers' Observed Responsiveness During Play with their Children: A Double-blind Within-subject Experiment*. Psychoneuroendocrinology 21:10, 1426-8.

Napthali, S. (2003). *Buddhism for Mothers: A Calm Approach to Caring for Yourself and Your Children*. Crows Nest, Australia: Allen & Unwin.

Neill, J. T. (2001). *Adventure Education and Resilience: The Double-edged Sword*. Journal of Adventure Education and Outdoor Learning 1:2, 35-42.

Nelsen, J. (2006). *Positive Discipline*, 4th ed. New York, Random House.

Newton, R. P. (2008). *The Attachment Connection: Parenting a Secure & Confident Child Using the Science of Attachment Theory*. Oakland, New Harbinger Publications

Pierrehumbert, B. et al. (2010). *Oxytocin Response to an Experimental Psychosocial Challenge in Adults Exposed to Traumatic Experiences During Childhood or Adolescence*. Neuroscience 166:1, 168-77.

Pipher, M. (2006). *Writing to Change the World*. New York, Penguin Group.

Placone, P. M. (2001). *A Curriculum for Mindful Parenting: A Model Development Dissertation*. Cincinnati, The Union Institute & University.

Placone, P. M. (2009). *Growing Happy Children with Your*

Smile. Retrieved December 10, 2010 from www.mindfulparenthappychild.com/growing-happy-children-with-your-smile/

Ramachandran, V. (2006). *Mirror Neurons and The Brain in a Vat.* Retrieved April 28, 2010 from Edge: The Third Culture www.edge.org/3rd_culture/ramachandran06/ramachandran06_index.html

Ramel, W. G. (2004). *The Effects of Mindfulness Meditation on Cognitive Processes and Affect in Patients with Past Depression.* Cognitive Therapy and Research 28:4, 433-455.

Resnick, M. D. (1997). *Protecting Adolescents from Harm: Findings from the National Longitudinal Study on Adolescent Health.* Journal of the American Medical Association 278:10, 823-32.

Riem, M. M. et al. (2010). *Oxytocin Receptor Gene and Depressive Symptoms Associated with Physiological Reactivity to Infant Crying.* Social Cognitive and Affective Neuroscience. First published online April 16.

Rifkin, J. (2009). *The Empathic Civilization: The Race to Global Consciousness in a World in Crisis.* New York, Jeremy P. Tarcher-Penguin.

Robertson, J. (1952). *Film: A Two Year-Old Goes to Hospital.* Online at: www.robertsonfilms.info

Roizen, M. F. (2006). *You On a Diet: The Owner's Manual for Waist Management.* New York, Free Press.

Ross, H. E. et al. (2009). *Characterization of the Oxytocin System Regulating Affiliative Behavior in Female Prairie Voles.* Neuroscience 162:4, 892-903.

Rothwell, N. (2006). *The Different Facets of Mindfulness.*

Journal of Rational-Emotive & Cognitive-Behavior Therapy 24:1, 79-86.

Rushdie, S. (1991). *One Thousand Days in a Balloon*. In S. Rusdie, Imaginary Homelands: Essays and Criticism. London, Penguin Books 430-39.

Schore, A. (1997). *Affect Regulation and the Origin of the Self*. Hillsdale, NJ, Erlbaum.

Schore, A. (2003). *Affect Regulation and the Repair of the Self*. New York, Norton.

Segal, Z. V. et al. (2002). *Mindfulness-Based Cognitive Therapy for Depression: A New Approach to Preventing Relapse*. New York, The Guilford Press.

Seligman, M. E. (2002). *Authentic Happiness: Using the New Positive Psychology to Realize Your Potential for Lasting Fulfillment*. New York, Free Press.

Seligman, M. E. (2006). *Learned Optimism: How to Change Your Mind and Your Life*. New York, Vintage Books.

Shamay-Tsoory, S. G. et al. (2009). *Intranasal Administration of Oxytocin Increases Envy and Schadenfreude (Gloating)*. Biological Psychiatry 66:9, 864-70.

Shimoff, M. (2008). *Happy for No Reason: 7 Steps to Being Happy from the Inside Out*. New York, Free Press.

Siegel, D. J. (1999). *The Developing Mind: How Relationships and The Brain Interact to Shape Who We Are*. New York, Guilford Press.

Siegel, D. J. and Hartzell, M. (2003). *Parenting from the Inside Out: How a Deeper Self-Understanding Can Help You Raise Children Who Thrive*. New York, Jeremy P. Tarcher-Penguin.

Siegel, D. J. (2007). *The Mindful Brain: Reflection and Attunement in the Cultivation of Well-Being*. New York, W.

W. Norton.

Siegel, D. J. (2009). *Mindful Awareness, Mindsight, and Neural Integration*. The Humanistic Psychologist 37:2, 137-58.

Siegel, D. J. (2010). *Mindsight: The New Science of Personal Transformation*. New York, Bantam Books.

Singer, T. et al. (2004). *Empathy for Pain Involves the Affective but not Sensory Components of Pain*. Science 303:55661, 1157-62.

Snowdon, C. T. et al. (2010). *Variation in Oxytocin is Related to Variation in Affiliative Behavior in Monogamous, Pairbonded Tamarins*. Hormones and Behavior 58, 614-18.

Stibich, Mark. (2009). *Top 10 Health Benefits of a Good Night's Sleep: Why Sleep Matters to You*. About.com Guide. Updated May 2008.

Strathearn, L. et al. (2009). *Adult Attachment Predicts Maternal Brain and Oxytocin Response to Infant Cues*. Neuropsychopharmacology 34, 2655-66.

Suzuki, S. (1970/1998). *Zen Mind, Beginner's Mind: Informal Talks on Zen Meditation and Practice*. New York, Weatherhill.

Tanaka, K. Osako, Y. and Yuri, K. (2010). *Juvenile Social Experience Regulates Central Neuropeptides Relevant to Emotional and Social Behaviors*. Neuroscience 166:4, 1036-42.

Taylor, J. G. (1999). *The Race for Consciousness*. Cambridge, MA: The MIT Press.

The Dalai Lama, and Cutler, H. C. (1998). *The Art of Happiness: A Handbook for Living*. New York, Riverhead Books.

Tronich, E. (2007). *Still Face Experiment*. Retrieved 2009

from www.youtube.com/watch?v=apzXGEbZht0

Yapko, Michael D. (1999). *Hand Me Down Blues: How to Stop Depression from Spreading in Families.* New York, St. Martin Press.

Yapko, M. D. (2009). *Depression Is Contagious: How the Most Common Mood Disorder is Spreading Around the World and How to Stop It.* New York, Free Press.

Yi-Yuan T. et al. (2007, October 27). *Short-term Meditation Training Improves Attention and Self-regulation.* PNAS.org. www.ncbi.nlm.nih.gov/pmc/articles/PMC2040428/

Yi-Yuan T. et al. (2009, April 12). *Central and Autonomic Nervous System Interaction is Altered by Short-Term Meditation.* Retrieved January 13, 2010 from PNAS.org: http://pnas.org/cgi/doi/10.1073/pnas.0904031106

Zak, P. J., Stanton, A. A. and Ahmadi, S. (2007). *Oxytocin Increases Generosity in Humans.* PLoS ONE. 2:11,1128.

Zappe. J. (2010). *Glassdoor List the Best (Yes, Best!) Places to Work.* Retrieved December 15, 2010 from www.glassdoor.com

Index

Autopilot, 10
Avoidant attachment, causes of, 61
Awareness
  benefits of, 18
  emotional, 99-100
  of family legacy, 38-39
  of family patterns, 194-196
  mindful, 201-202
  of senses, 80-81, 186-187
  windows of, 75, 79-80, 185-189
Awareness of body
  cultivation of, 88-89
  importance of, 83-85
  for physiological balance, 84
  self check for, 89-90
  single dad's case, 85-88
Awareness training, goals of, 185

B
Balance
  mental and emotional, 14
  TINGLE for recovery of, 128
Blaming, 49
Bonding, oxytocin in, 2-3
Brain
  anatomy and function of, 21, 27-28
  automatic activity in, 10
  change in structure and function of, 27-28
  of child, 29
  childhood prewiring of, 36-37
  compassion effect on, 254
  described, 27
  environment influence on, 97

influencing structures and functions of, 117
Breathing
  during meditation, 209
  during time-out, 130, 134

C
Calm in middle of storm, 4-5
Central nervous system, compassion effect on, 254
Challenges
  engaging, 229-230
  rehearsal for, 150
Change
  in brain structure and function, 27-28
  intentional, 12
  as possibility, 8, 25
  self-awareness and, 260
  transformation and, 65
  world need for, 260
Child
  benefit of discipline and, 176
  communication of needs by, 69-70
  conditioning of, 37, 39
  needs of, 28-29, 69-70
Child rearing as gardening, 69
Childhood, victim of, 48-49
Choice, emotional awareness and, 103
Closeness, with mindful parenting, 4
Commitment
  to daily practice, 192
  renewal of, 159
Communication
  attentiveness in, 170-172,

E

Effort, in being present, 67
Emotional awareness, 99-100
  benefits of, 102-103
  problems of, 103-104
Emotional contagion, 114-115
Emotional reactivity
  identification of causes of,
    104-105
  working through, 105-106
Emotional readiness, for
  relationship repair, 165-166
Emotional regulation
  secure attachment and, 62
Emotions
  attunement to, 111
  awareness of, 99-103
  expression of, in family of
    origin, 107-108
  learned management of, 107
  loss of control and, 104
  memories and, 104
Observer of, 100
  past and, 100
  positive, benefits of, 98
  response to child's, 108
  sense of other's, 111
  stuffing, 108-109
  unawareness of, 103
Empathy
  benefit of, 122
  communication of, 123
  defined, 122
  development of, 123, 246-251
  enhancement of, 122
Three Degrees Rule and, 258
Enjoyment, with mindful
  parenting, 4

Environment
  genetic alteration and, 259
  influence on brain structures,
    97
  relational, 41
Equanimity, in being present, 66
Explicit memory vs. implicit
  memory, 92
Expressiveness, 227
  as mirror of interest and
    feelings, 172

F

Family
  awareness benefits to, 10-11
  multigenerational
    transmission of negativity
    in, 40
Family health, markers of, 41
Family legacy
  assessment of, 48
  changing, 199-201
  chosen vs. inherited, 40-41
  heirlooms in, personal
    inventory of, 194-195
  judgmental attitude, 26
  reflection on, 42-43
  of resilience, 152
  rewriting your story, 43
Family of origin
  emotion in, 107-108
  historical questions about,
    45-48
  interaction in, 42-43
  reaction in, 43
Family patterns, awareness of,
  41, 194-196
Family story, visualization of, 44

Family tree. See also Genogram
    studying, 197-199
Fear, turning down, 249-251
Feelings. See Emotions
Freedom, discipline for, 174-176

G

Genes, alteration of, 259
Genogram, description of, 44
Getting out the Door scenario,
    self-intervention in, 127-
    128
Goal
    affirmation of, 8
    in plan of action, 135-136
Gratefulness, 6
Grounding, in self-intervention,
    132, 134

H

Heirlooms. See also Family
    legacy
    personal inventory of, 194-
    195
    reflection on, in parent-child
    interaction, 42-43

I

Impatience, patience vs., 66
Implicit memory
    encoding and contents of, 37-
    38
    origin of, 37
    vs. explicit memory, 92
Individuality, I, 251
Inhale-exhale. See also
    Breathing
    in self-intervention, 130

Insecure-ambivalent
    attachment, 60
Insecure-avoidant attachment,
    60
Insights
    from genogram, 44
    from self-awareness, 12
    from self-observation, 13-14
Intention
    in mindful parenting, 55
    renewal of, 160
    setting with affirmations, 7-8
Interaction
    adult-child, 55-56
    in family of origin, 42-43

J

Joining with child, 228
    in communication, 172-173,
    228
    in plan of action, 135, 137
    ways of, 172-173
Journaling, 6
Judgment
    "better than/less-than"
        attitude, 22, 25
    defined, 22
    effects of, 22-23
    evidence of, 67
    in families, 23
    impact on children, 23-24
    as learned behavior, 26
    in media, 22-23
    negative, 132
    observation of in self and
        children, 26
    of self, 24, 26

observation and imitation, 116

sense of internal world of another and, 116-117

Mirroring back, 170-171, 174

Mistakes, owning, 166-167

N

Naming, in self-intervention, 130-132

Needs of child
from adults, 29
child's communication of, 69-70
failure to respond to, 59
responsibility for, 70

Negativity
multigenerational transmission of, 40
of news media, 249-250

Neurobiology interpersonal, 254-255

Neurons, 27

Neurol pathways, 27-28, 37, 39

News media
judgment in, 22-23
negative impact of, 249-250

No excuses, forms of, 167

Nonjudgment
in being present, 67-68
practicing, 67-68

Nonreactivity, benefits of, 20-21

O

Observation. See also Self-observation of judgment, 26
practicing, 216-217
of self and experience, 5-6,

13-14

Observer, 217-219
defined, 12, 13
describing the present moment, 16-18, 190-191
in discounting self to acceptance of self, 14-15
of emotions, 100
inner voice for, 218
over-the-top reaction and, 14
view from self-observation deck, 15-16

Orientation
I, 251-253
we, 252-253

Owning it
examples of, 166
taking responsibility for, 166-167

Oxytocin
in biology of bonds, 3
effects of, 2-3

P

Parent-child connection. See also Attachment
communication in, 169-173
five R's for, 147-168
healthy, 57-58
maintenance of, 147
secure attachment and, 58-64

Parent-child experiences, effect on children, 58-59

Parenting
cultivating inner self for, 54-55
as gardening, 53-54, 64-65

Sound, awareness of, 82, 186
STONE for relationship repair
  no excuses in, 167
  owning it in, 166-167
  showing up in, 163-165
  timing in, 165-166
Strategy, in plan of action, 135-137
Stress
  financial cost of, 153
  in parenting, 20-21
  resilience and, 152-153, 153
Survival instinct, in children, 69

T
Taste, awareness of, 81, 187
Teenagers, bridging
  disconnections with, 173
Thinking. See Thoughts and
  thinking
Thirty-second connection
  benefits of, 174
  importance of, 173
Thoughts and thinking
  automatic reactions and, 94
  awareness of, 90-91, 95
  effects of, 91
  internal dialogue, 91
  learning to work with, 93-94
  minding, 92-94
  "monkey mind" and, 93
  personal experience of
    negative assumptions,
    91-92
Three Degrees of Influence
  Rule, 257-258
Time
  in being present, 68

conscious use of, 69
mindfulness and, 7
Time-out for parents
  as learning opportunity for
    child, 140
  mental and physical, 129
  for renewal, 159
  rules for, 129
  in self-intervention, 129-131
Timing, in relationship repair,
  165-166
TINGLE method, of self-
  intervention, 203-205
Touch
  in attentiveness, 170, 172
  awareness of, 81-82, 187
  development and, 59-60
Transformation, description of,
  65
Trauma, oxytocin system and, 3
TV, negative impact of, 249-250

U
Unplugging negative media,
  250

V
Values, development of healthy,
  57
Victim of childhood, 48-49

W
Walking meditation, 7
Water, body's need for, 86
Wounds from childhood
  transmission to child, 40
  unresolved, 43

About the Author

Pilar M. Placone, Ph.D. is a licensed marriage and family therapist whose twenty years of practice is dedicated to bringing clients a renewed sense of hope and fulfillment. Dr. Placone works toward achieving this goal by deeply attuning to the needs of each client using a wide variety of healing modalities, which include classical and modern psychology, interpersonal neurobiology, and Eastern meditative practices.

Dr. Placone founded the *Mindful Parent Happy Child* programs in order to provide a more holistic and comprehensive set of behavioral tools for both parents and therapists. She is also a member of the Interpersonal Neurobiology seminar group, which is facilitated by Dr. Dan Siegel, author of *The Developing Mind, Parenting from the inside Out*, and *Mindsight*.

Dr. Placone is available for talks, education, and training in the area of mindful parenting. She has an ongoing schedule of classes and workshops. If you would like to incorporate *Mindful Parent Happy Child* principles into your home, organization, or professional practice, please contact Dr. Placone through her website: www. MindfulParentHappyChild.com.